# RF-8 CRUSADER
## UNITS OVER CUBA
## AND VIETNAM

SERIES EDITOR: TONY HOLMES

OSPREY COMBAT AIRCRAFT · 12

# RF-8 CRUSADER
## OVER CUBA
## AND VIETNAM

Peter Mersky

**Front cover**
On 17 August 1966, Lt Andre Coltrin of VFP-63 Det G flew an extremely hazardous photo-reconnaissance mission to the MiG base at Kep in North Vietnam. Escorted by Air Force exchange pilot Capt Wil Abbott of VF-111 in an F-8C, Coltrin threaded RF-8G BuNo 146871 AH 601 through the mountains north of Haiphong, then headed west toward Hanoi and Kep. North Vietnamese gunners in the mountains were actually firing down at the American aircraft as the Crusader pilots tried to take advantage of the mountains all around them in an effort to mask enemy radar. At times Coltrin took his flight *down* so low that later, the exposed film showed clothes lines full of laundry.

Nearing Hanoi, the Crusaders were again taken under intense enemy fire, with many flak bursts detonating so close to Coltrin's RF-8 that the jet physically shook in the clear blue sky – the bursts were white, denoting 37 mm AAA, or black puffs with red centres for the bigger 57 mm rounds. Nearly every warning light in Coltrin's cockpit lit up, including the gauges for the vital fuel and hydraulic systems, as the flak peppered his aircraft.

Having completed his photographic runs and left the flak-filled skies behind him, Coltrin pulled up to allow his escort pilot to visually check his jet over, and finding he could still control the damaged RF-8, Coltrin made it back to his carrier with the assistance of an A-4 tanker. He received the Distinguished Flying Cross for this mission, which was one of three DFCs he received for his combat service (*cover artwork by Iain Wyllie*)

**Dedication**
**For the 'Peeping Toms' and the 'Hawks', and the 'Andrews RF-8G Mafia'**

First published in Great Britain in 1999
by Osprey Publishing
Elms Court, Chapel Way
Botley, Oxford, OX2 9LP, UK

ISBN 1 85532 782 1

Edited by Tony Holmes
Page design by TT Designs, T & B Truscott
Cover Artwork by Iain Wyllie
Aircraft Profiles by Tom Tullis
Figure Artwork by Mike Chappell
Scale Drawings by Mark Styling

Origination by Valhaven Ltd, Isleworth, UK
Printed in Hong Kong

99 00 01 02 03   10 9 8 7 6 5 4 3 2 1

EDITOR'S NOTE
To make this best-selling series as authoritative as possible, the editor would be extremely interested in hearing from any individual who may have relevant photographs, documentation or first-hand experiences relating to the elite pilots, and their aircraft, of the various theatres of war. Any material used will be fully credited to its original source. Please write to Tony Holmes at 10 Prospect Road, Sevenoaks, Kent, TN13 3UA, Great Britain.

ACKNOWLEDGEMENTS
Besides the many RF-8 drivers whose experiences are described herein, I would like to thank the following people for their help and support: Todd Baker and Roy Grossnick of the Naval Aviation History Office; Dr Ed Marolda of the Naval Historical Center; Daniel Crawford of the Marine Corps Historical Center; Hill Goodspeed of the National Museum of Naval Aviation; Dave Donald of Aerospace Publishing Ltd; Angelo Collura of the Defense PoW/MIA Office; and Norman Polmar.

# CONTENTS

# INTRODUCTION

A classic approach view of the USS *Franklin D Roosevelt* (CVA-42) taken by the forward-fire camera in an RF-8G's station one (directly below the nose) in November 1969. The white 'bar' at the extreme end of the flight deck is the rounddown. The LSOs can just be seen on their platform on the aft port side, and above them are the landing lights, which play such a crucial part in each approach

Only a few high-performance fighters have enjoyed simultaneously important combat careers, the secondary role usually being in an area for which they were never intended. High speed usually suggests the tactical-reconnaissance arena. The Vickers-Supermarine Spitfire, Lockheed P-38 Lightning and North American P-51 Mustang served well in this important, but decidedly less glamorous, area during World War 2 – oddly, the other major powers seldom used their fighters for reconnaissance.

Postwar reconnaissance fighters included the Royal Air Force's Meteor series (particularly the FR 9), the US Navy's Grumman F9F Panther and McDonnell F2H Banshee and the US Air Force's Republic RF-84F Thunderflash and Lockheed RF-80.

RF-8G BuNo 146897 takes off in full afterburner from NAS Miramar. This remanufactured A-model from VFP-63 displays the common *EYES OF THE FLEET* bulkhead marking on the raised wing. Having survived the Vietnam conflict, this particular aircraft was finally lost whilst operating with VFP-63 Det 4, as part of CVW-6, aboard USS *Independence* (CV-62) on 9 June 1981

An RF-8A from VMCJ-2 taxies up the flight deck after a trap. Although Marine Corps RF-8 pilots were, after all, naval aviators, and were required to maintain their carrier qualifications, many seldom saw a carrier. In a few months this aircraft and pilot would be flying missions from NAS Guántanamo during the 1962 Cuban Crisis. Remanufactured into an RF-8G, this particular aircraft (BuNo 145646) was lost some 17 years later whilst serving with VFP-63 Det 2 during cruise work-ups aboard *Coral Sea* on 13 October 1979 (*Harold Austin*)

Vought's world-beating F8U Crusader, which resurrected the struggling pioneer company's fortune almost single-handedly, seemed an ideal candidate for major redesign into a fast tactical-reconnaissance platform to essentially replace the Panther and Banshee. It had attracted national attention in July 1957 when Marine Maj John H Glenn flew from California to New York in three hours and twenty-three minutes, averaging 725.55 miles per hour (Mach 1.1).

While the fighter-Crusader began its fleet introduction in late 1956, 32nd production F8U-1 (the pre-1962 designation) BuNo 141363 was drastically altered forward of the wing. The fighter's four 20 mm internal cannon were deleted, the slim forward fuselage broadened and its belly flattened to accommodate a suite of Chicago Aerial cameras. Early-build F8U-1Ps (as the early designation system called the photo-recce version) carried a variety of vertical and oblique platforms, plus three separate – the trimetogen arrangement – cameras which used overlapping photography to give horizon-to-horizon coverage. Later, the KA-66 and KA-68 pan cameras gave true panoramic photography, being located in Station 2 – there were four camera positions in the photo-Crusader.

Station 1 was located directly below the cockpit, a prominent fairing housing a camera that looked directly along the jet's flight path at a 45° angle. This positioning was excellent for obtaining approach imagery to a target, and became one of the RF-8's most dependable cameras. Station 1 could also be altered to carry a 16 mm motion picture camera, although this was rarely used.

Besides Station 2, with its pan camera, the RF-8 included Stations 3 and 4 with vertically- and obliquely-mounted cameras that could look either directly below the aircraft, or out the side windows.

Film size was originally 70 mm (2.5-in square), but by 1967 the introduction of the RF-8G had seen the size enlarged to 4.5-in square.

The photo-Crusader's mission was intelligence-gathering. Without armament, and with a greatly increased internal fuel capacity, the RF-8 was a 'speedster', relying on surprise, pilot courage and skill – and perhaps a little luck – and supersonic dash speeds to get over the target, get the photos, and get out before enemy air defences could be brought to bear.

The F8U-1P made its first flight on 17 December 1956, and Vought's

A head-on view of a Marine RF-8A showing the distinctly 'boxy' look of the redesigned fuselage, which deleted the fighter's cannon for the suite of cameras. The pilot's viewfinder window is directly below the black nose cone. The fairing directly above the nosegear houses the forward-firing KA-45 camera – one of the aircraft's primary sensors

photo-bird joined the fleet with VFP-61 in September 1957. During this period, the Navy's reconnaissance squadrons went through a series of redesignations and re-equipment, but eventually by 1962 the two 'light-photographic' units were VFP-62 and -63, which covered responsibilities for the Atlantic and Pacific Fleets respectively. The Marine Corps used F8U-1Ps in composite reconnaissance squadrons (which had diverse, but related, tactical responsibilities), namely VMCJ-1, -2 and -3, whilst VMCJ-4 was a short-lived reserve unit.

Therefore, by mid-1962 the F8U-1P (which would be redesignated RF-8A in a major revamping of the American military numbering system that October) formed an important part of the naval aviation sea-going effort.

This 1959 photo of VMCJ-1 RF-8A BuNo 146861 shows the different cameras the photo-Crusader could carry, although not all at once. The deployed speedbrake, immediately forward of the main gear, appears to be striped. The Corps had a limited number of RF-8s, and this aircraft would find itself flying some of the earliest combat missions in Vietnam from several carriers in the latter half of 1964. Converted into an RF-8G, BuNo 146861 was lost in a non-combat-related accident in the South China Sea on 5 September 1972 whilst serving with VFP-63 Det 1 aboard *Hancock*. A second Crusader from CVW-21 (F-8J BuNo 150229 from VF-24) was also lost during a non-combat sortie on this day – both pilots were recovered

Because of its large internal fuel tanks, the RF-8 seldom needed to refuel in the air, but it never hurt to practice. These two VMCJ-2 RF-8Gs are seen receiving from a KC-130 during a stateside training mission

# CUBAN CRISIS

The photo-Crusader's first operational test came in the mid-autumn of 1962, and involved both Navy and Marine RF-8As. USAF U-2 reconnaissance flights had brought back indications, but not incontestable proof, that the Soviets had introduced intermediate-range ballistic missiles(IRBMs) into their client state, the island of communist Cuba. On 13 October, in conjunction with continued USAF flights, VFP-62 and Marine squadron VMCJ-2 were ordered to stand by at Naval Air Station (NAS) Cecil Field, near Jacksonville.

The RF-8As were needed for low-level high-speed runs to confirm the earlier U-2 photos that only showed earth moving and unconfirmed construction activity. Cuban agents reported information about possible missile bases, and the US government wanted a closer look. A high-flying U-2 might take only one to two frames a minute, but an RF-8 travelling at 600 knots at 5000 ft took several frames a second. No only was the coverage that much greater, it was also more detailed.

While VFP-62 scrambled to get detachments to carriers in case the 'big ships' went on a war footing, its land-based 'home squadron' prepared for operations over Cuba. Four Marine pilots were assigned to VFP-62 to provide additional resources and fly the Navy squadron's RF-8s. The flights duly began on 23 October 1962 under the codename *Blue Moon*, six aircraft overflying three targets – two RF-8s apiece. Two aircraft always flew per sortie. Fourteen flights were made on 27 October, which proved to be the greatest number during the entire operation.

The RF-8As made two flights daily from NAS Key West, completing low-level high-speed dashes over the heavily-defended island before landing back at NAS Jacksonville, where the Crusaders' film was downloaded and rushed for processing and interpretation at the Fleet Air Photo Lab (FAPL) owned by VFP-62. After their film was downloaded, the RF-8As returned to Cecil Field, which was just a short

Cdr William Ecker dismounts from his RF-8A after a mission over Cuba. This photograph was taken sometime after the squadron had received the first ever peacetime Navy Unit Commendation on 26 November 1962 – note the ribbon painted on the Crusader's nose. The forward-fire camera bay is already open, as is the number-three bay door behind the plane captain assisting his skipper

9

Cdr Ecker gives his initial impressions of the mission. A career naval pilot, Ecker had seen combat in F4U-1D Corsairs during World War 2 as a member of VBF-10 aboard USS *Intrepid* (CV-11). Note his large oxygen mask with bayonet fittings. The bullets on his chest bandoleer can just be seen between the mask and the right shoulder strap of his torso harness

Another dead chicken means another successful mission over Cuba. Each RF-8A received a caricature of Cuban Premier Fidel Castro – note the he is wearing a baseball uniform, which refers to the Cuban nation's passion for the game – and a dead chicken marking for each mission. Castro's fear of being poisoned in New York during a state visit, and his demand for a freshly killed chicken, prompted the latter marking

Above: Still in full flight gear, Cdr Ecker leans over the light table to run through mission film with photo interpreters and other interested officers at the Jacksonville photo lab. Note Ecker's ammunition belt, characteristically worn across the chest

Below: A page from Cdr Ecker's flight log, showing some of the October missions over Cuba. Note that although the designation system for the Navy's aircraft had changed that month, the yeoman responsible for inscribing this vital piece of a pilot's record still refers to the RF-8A as F8U-1P

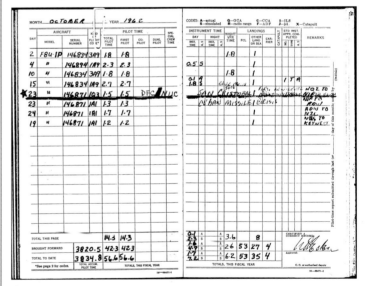

flight away from Jacksonville, for maintenance. They then returned to Key West for the next missions. Over a six-week period, these operations saw RF-8s bring back more than 160,000 negatives.

The Missile Crisis was in full swing when the US Navy instituted a naval blockade, challenging the Soviets' continued movement to and from Cuba. The world has never, before or since, seemed so close to nuclear war. Finally, after a week of diplomatic furore, the Soviets agreed to dismantle the missile installations and remove them from Cuba.

While the delicate negotiations continued, so did the *Blue Moon*

GA 910 (BuNo 146871) taxies in at NAS Jacksonville after a mission in late 1962, with squadron CO, Cdr William Ecker at the controls. Like many of the Cuban Crisis RF-8As, this aircraft was later remanufactured as a G-model and saw heavy action in Vietnam with the VFP-63 det on board *Oriskany* in 1966, amongst several other TF 77 cruises. It was finally lost in an operational accident whilst flying with VFP-63 on 2 December 1976

President John F Kennedy, second from left, awards VFP-62 the first peacetime Navy Unit Commendation on 26 November 1962. Cdr William Ecker is seen shaking the president's hand after accepting the award for his unit

flights. Recovering at Jacksonville after a mission, each Crusader would receive another 'dead chicken' marking below its cockpit to denote the successful completion of the flight. This marking referred to a comical episode involving Cuban Premier Castro who, on an early visit to New York City in 1960, demanded a live chicken be killed and cooked for him on the spot to prevent someone trying to assassinate him by poisoning his food.

In addition to the 'chicken' markings, every Crusader had the phrase 'Smile, you're on Candid Camera' painted on the lower fuselage surface immediately in front of the Station 1 camera blister.

The chronology of RF-8A sorties per day during *Blue Moon* was as follows:

| | |
|---|---|
| 23 October - three flown | 7 November - four flown |
| 25 October - ten flown | 8 November - four flown |
| 27 October - fourteen flown | 9 November - six flown |
| 29 October - two flown | 10 November - four flown |
| 1 November - two flown | 11 November - four flown |
| 2 November - two flown | 12 November - four flown |
| 3 November - two flown | 13 November - six flown |
| 5 November - six flown | 15 November - two flown |
| 6 November - two flown | |

No Navy flights were made from 15 November 1962 through to the final sortie on 5 June 1963.

The 12 regular squadron pilots that participated in *Blue Moon* each received the Distinguished Flying Cross, and VFP-62 itself received the first peacetime Navy Unit Commendation, which was personally presented to the unit's CO by President John F Kennedy when he visited the squadron at Key West on 26 November 1962. The four Marine aviators who flew *Blue Moon* missions received their DFCs from CINCLANT, Adm Robert L Dennison, at a separate ceremony in Jacksonville. Unfortunately, the Marines were not eligible for the unit commendation because they were not technically part of VFP-62.

Capt (later Lieutenant-General) John Hudson was one of the four

One of four VMCJ-2 Marine aviators assigned to VFP-62, Capt John I Hudson (right) shakes hands with Cdr Ecker after completing yet another sortie over Cuba. The humorous dead-chicken marking is prominently displayed between them. Hudson went on to enjoy a full career with the Corps, commanding F-4 squadrons and eventually retiring as a lieutenant general (three stars)

Harold Austin, affectionately known as 'Hoss', poses on his photo-Crusader on the day of his permanent promotion to captain – the pilot almost certainly received his nickname because of his resemblance to television actor Dan Blocker, who played the character of 'Hoss' Cartwright in the popular Western series *Bonanza*. Barely visible on the left collar of his flightsuit is the metal insignia of a sergeant (pay grade E-5), from which he was commissioned. On this important day, he decided he wanted his promotion dramatically documented on film

Marine RF-8 pilots assigned to VFP-62 during the crisis. At first, he and his squadronmates flew at 200 ft over Cuba, which was considerably lower than on subsequent missions, which were performed at a height of 1000 ft. The initial low altitude sorties produced disappointingly 'soft' photos because of the salt sea spray thrown up as the Crusader pilots tried to fly below Cuban radar. On subsequent *Blue Moon* missions, pilots would pop up to 1000 ft at 480 knots, overfly their targets, then shut off their cameras and descend once again to an egress height of 200 ft. Hudson still vividly recalls the heavy Cuban flak which nearly shot down several RF-8As.

Along with his three Marine Corps buddies, Hudson had initially undertaken the two-hour flight from his base at Cherry Point, in North Carolina, to join VFP-62 at Key West on 19 October. On 10 November two of the Marine pilots flew a mission to commemorate the USMC's 187th birthday, one of the jets involved being RF-8A BuNo 145611 which included this flight as one of five consecutive sorties completed during the crisis.

Although VFP-62 performed the bulk of the Crusader overflights once the Cuban situation had come to a head, Marine RF-8s from a small VMCJ-2 detachment based at the large US Navy facility at Guántanamo ('Gitmo'), on the Cuban mainland, also provided an interesting sidelight during the stand-off.

In the two years prior to the crisis, VMCJ-2 had been performing electronic-surveillance flights with specially-equipped Douglas F3D Skyknights – this large twin-engined straight-winged jet, which later in its long career would become an important platform for gathering ELINT (electronic intelligence) in Vietnam, had made its combat debut a decade earlier during the Korean War, when Marine F3Ds had accounted for a number of night kills, including six MiG-15s (see *Osprey Aircraft of the Aces 4 - Korean War Aces* for further details).

The Marine F3Ds would take off from nearby Caribbean airfields such as those on Jamaica or in the Bahamas in the early pre-dawn hours, then fly well off the Cuban coast enticing Cuban radar to show itself. The Cubans usually obliged, and the Marines always brought back a lot of intelligence, which took several weeks to analyse. The Skyknights also had direct radio

The men of the forgotten 'Gitmo' contingent pose by one of their aircraft, prominently displaying their unit banner. Harold Austin and Capt Gary Hintz (second and third from left, front row) relied on these people to keep their RF-8As up and ready during the crisis

Capts Gary Hintz (left) and Harold Austin (right) pose by one of two RF-8As from the VMCJ-2 det at Guántanamo. The two aviators flew recon missions during the crisis, including several at night. Note their bandoleers and sidearm holsters. Hintz retired as a colonel, while Austin retired as a major and later became a Wesleyan minister

links with the US Joint Chiefs of Staff (JCS), even though these missions were flown in a complete radio blackout.

With the onset of the Cuban Crisis, however, and in addition to the seconded pilots and groundcrews sent to the larger VFP-62 effort, a two-jet detachment flew to Guántanamo, staging through Boca Chica, in Florida. Young Crusader driver Capt Harold M Austin Jr was the squadron logistics officer at the time, and he was somewhat miffed at having to stay behind to ensure that the det firstly departed Cherry Point in good shape and then arrived safely in Cuba. He did eventually join the det, however, which had been administratively detached from the squadron and reassigned to the group at 'Gitmo' soon after its arrival.

Although the main reconnaissance operation was flown by the combined VFP-62/VMCJ-2 group, the 'Gitmo' Marines did also fly missions – especially several night photo runs. Unfortunately, the man in charge at 'Gitmo' was a non-aviator colonel who did not fully understand air operations, and this quickly became apparent to the Crusader pilots as the following episode shows.

In the wake of the shootdown of a U-2 on 27 October, Capt Austin was tasked with providing high-altitude pin-point photography of the missile site that had hit the high-flying USAF aircraft. The JCS suggested that the RF-8 should fly at 35,000 ft, which not only put it right in the missile envelope, but would also have a detrimental effect on the photographs taken. Austin told the 'ground-pounder' colonel that a high-speed low-level run would give much better coverage, and would also keep him out of the missile's envelope.

The colonel replied that Austin should not worry – there would be four fighters offshore monitoring the photo jet's progress. Of course, there would have been little the escort could have done against a missile except to call out where it hit the reconnaissance Crusader, and where, and if, Austin had ejected. Austin's objections fell on deaf ears, and he flew the mission 'very scared'.

An amusing story that highlights the sometimes intense inter-service rivalry during the crisis involves the RF-8 cameras manufactured by

RF-8A BuNo 145646 (which is also shown in the introduction as CY 5 aboard a carrier at an earlier stage in its career, indicating just how often side numbers change) flies over Guántanamo in 1962 just before the crisis flared up. Note the rabbit logo of *Playboy* magazine, which the squadron appropriated to go with its 'Playboy' callsign. They used the callsign throughout Vietnam and into the 1980s, as VMAQ-2. However, political correctness eventually made them give it up – pity

Chicago Aerial Industries. The USAF had been having trouble with its McDonnell RF-101A Voodoo (counterpart of the photo-Crusader), which was also a derivative of an original fighter variant of the 1950s – the large and fast F-101A was a single-seat long-range fighter that boasted an impressive straight speed performance, but never flew satisfactorily in its intended role. The RF-101 enjoyed a somewhat more successful career, and saw considerable action during the first five years of the Vietnam War.

However, during those anxious weeks of October 1962, the temperamental photo-Voodoos were down more often than up, and the fact that the jets' cameras were not ready for such a real-world test, simply pointed to the service's unpreparedness.

In an act of desperation, the Air Force asked Chicago Aerial if it could purchase the KA-45 cameras that were an integral part of the RF-8A's suite – the KA-45 was one of three specific camera models fitted in four stations within the Crusader's large fuselage, being mounted in station 1 beneath the RF-8A's large nose intake, looking forward along the aircraft's flight path. This dependable camera gave an excellent view of entry points for bomb runs.

Chicago Aerial told the Air Force that although 22 cameras were ready for shipment, they were already assigned to their Navy purchasers. Ultimately, the colourful USAF Chief of Staff, Gen Curtis LeMay, got involved in the deal and, leaning heavily on the Navy for past favours, got the admiral in charge to split the order with the Air Force.

The manufacturer installed the cameras in Voodoos of the USAF's 363rd Tactical Reconnaissance Wing at Shaw AFB, in South Carolina, and finally six RF-101s were ready to assume their roles at MacDill AFB in Tampa, Florida. In truth, however, although the Air Force received a lot of favourable publicity, including being featured in *Life* magazine, its RF-101s sat out most of the vital week of 23-28 October because of problems with their camera systems.

Two Marine RF-8As of VMCJ-2 fly form over the Caribbean during 1962. Unlike many other long-lived tactical jets, the RF-8 was never encumbered with underwing fuel tanks or other paraphernalia. And only two ventral fuselage strakes were added to the aircraft for high-speed directional stability when 73 A-models were upgraded to RF-8G specs in the mid- to late-1960s. The aircraft nearest the camera (BuNo 146863) survived many years of service with VFP-63 until retired (as PP 646) to the 'desert boneyard' at Davis-Monthan AFB, in Arizona, on 15 December 1980 – it is still part of the Aerospace Maintenance and Regeneration Center (AMARC) inventory today. BuNo 15636, however, was lost during a routine flight in the USA on 1 August 1972

# EARLY OPERATIONS IN SOUTH-EAST ASIA

By the time American participation in the growing conflict in South-East Asia took a more active role in the late summer of 1964, the Crusader was firmly established in the Atlantic and Pacific Fleets in both the fighter and reconnaissance roles. F-8 squadrons and detachments served worldwide. Yet, with the exception of the 1962 Cuban Missile Crisis, and a few isolated, hard-to-document, encounters with Cuban and other communist aircraft, the Crusader had not seen combat. Vietnam would change that.

There was talk of a mission flown over communist China in the early 1960s where an RF-8A, escorted by a fighter – maybe from carrier *Ticonderoga*'s (CVA-19) air wing – penetrated Chinese airspace, only to be shot down by anti-aircraft fire. The rumour is hard to confirm but is, nonetheless, tantalising.

The events surrounding the war in Vietnam have been well documented in the last five years, and a retelling here is not necessary (a more detailed account of this important engagement, and of the F-8's career in Vietnam, appears in the companion volume *Osprey Combat Aircraft 7 - F-8 Crusader Units of the Vietnam War*). Suffice it to say that as the largely civil war in Vietnam, which had been partitioned in 1954, intensified, the US supported the South Vietnamese government not only with specific supplies and material, but with training and maintaining a large task force off the long Vietnamese coastline in the South China Sea.

The skittish F-8 demanded constant attention even after touchdown. Crosswinds and slender tyres made for some unpleasant post-landing incidents, as this shot of VFP-63 RF-8A BuNo 145641 attests to. The pilot ended the sortie in a drainage ditch after leaving the runway in July 1964. Quickly repaired, the jet was later converted into an RF-8G and eventually became the penultimate photo-Crusader lost when, on 19 July 1981, its pilot was forced to eject whilst serving with VFP-63 Det 2 during pre-*WestPac* cruise work-ups aboard *Coral Sea* – this was the second RF-8G lost by the det from CV-43 during work-ups in less than two years

A VMCJ-1 RF-8A (BuNo 146892) in mid-1964 – immediately before the unit's deployment to South Vietnam. RM 10 eventually went out to supplement the VFP-63 det aboard USS *Kitty Hawk* (CVA-63). This aircraft was later written off whilst flying as an RF-8G with VFP-63 on 15 July 1976

RM 14 (BuNo 146884) was an early casualty of the VMCJ-1 deployment to Da Nang, being lost during a non-combat-related flight on 22 August 1965

Before the climactic Gulf of Tonkin Incidents of early August 1964, American carriers had steamed north and south in support of various land-based operations. The main operation involved aerial reconnaissance using specially-configured RA-3B Skywarriors and RF-8As of VFP-63 detachments. Laos, which had been under direct Communist attack, was of special interest. Under the name *Team Yankee*, the Navy contributed its resources to a combined effort to both gather intelligence and show the North Vietnamese that South Vietnam was not alone.

To demonstrate American concern, Air Force and Navy reconnaissance aircraft began flying low-level photo runs over the Plaine des Jars and along the Laotian 'panhandle'. The *Kitty Hawk* (CVA-63) embarked three RF-8As and two RA-3Bs of VFP-63 and VAP-61, respectively. Eventually, with the addition of another RF-8 det from *Bon Homme Richard* (CVA-31) and aircraft from Marine squadron VMCJ-1, the *Kitty Hawk* photo contingent boasted ten pilots and eleven RF-8As. The photo-Crusader, and its operators, began a complicated series of detachments on board various ships as the Navy and Marine Corps strove to have a viable day reconnaissance force in theatre as soon as possible.

The arrival of VMCJ-1's

Seen here as a major, and the operations officer and XO of VMFA-122 in 1973, Denis Kiely flew some of the war's earliest photo-reconnaissance missions as a member of VMCJ-1 aboard the carrier *Kitty Hawk*. Like many of his cohorts, Kiely 'cross-pollinated' to a fighter unit in 1967, flying many in-country close air support missions with VMF(AW)-235 in F-8Es

With his engine still turning, this photo-recce pilot is directed into his carrier's hangar bay after completing a mission

Crusaders in South-East Asia marked the first use of Marine Corps fixed-wing jets in Vietnam, the five-pilot det having made its way from Iwakuni, Japan, to Cubi Point, in the Philippine Islands. 1Lts Denis Kiely, John Sledge and Alexander Carter and Capts Lloyd Draayer and Russ French then received orders to fly out to the carrier, where they met Lt Cdr Ben Cloud, the OINC of the carrier's photo detachment, and one of the Navy's few black aviators at the time. The 'Romeo-Mike' Crusaders (referring to the Marines' RM tailcode letters) landed aboard *Kitty Hawk* on 22 May 1964. Most of the young aviators had not seen a carrier since March, a few since the previous December. Regulations dictated no more than a six-month break to be properly qualified to land aboard ship, so the Marines were legal, but stretching it in this exacting arena.

Billeting was a minor problem aboard the crowded ship, and friction between the Marine det and the regular Navy ship's company initially cropped up. However, the Marines soon settled in and began flying train-

Photos of early Vietnam RF-8s in-theatre are rare, this view showing one such jet (RF-8A BuNo 146855 from VFP-63's Det F aboard *Constellation*) refuelling from an A-4C of VA-146 in August 1963 – less than a year before the first RF-8A was lost to enemy action. A survivor of countless Vietnam sorties, and later upgraded to G-model specs, this aircraft earned the dubious distinction of being the last Crusader to crash in Navy service when its pilot, reservist Cdr David Strong (XO of VFP-206), was forced to eject due to power loss soon after taking off from NAS Miramar on 11 March 1985

Two early RF-8As of VFP-63. Because neither jet carries the name of a CVA over the rear-fuselage *NAVY* marking, it is probable they are from the squadron's 'home guard' at Miramar. Note the differing applications of the serials on the fins of each RF-8, the painted rear fuselage area on the Crusader nearest the camera, and the fin band on the latter aircraft. BuNo 146832 was lost on 13 June 1963 during an operational flight in the USA, whilst BuNo 146898 remained in service until the mid-1980s, when it was retired and placed on display in the aircraft park alongside the battleship USS *Alabama* in Mobile, Alabama – the jet is on loan from the National Museum of Naval Aviation at NAS Pensacola, Florida

ing, followed by operational missions over Laos, sometimes in Navy Crusaders – the dets pooled their aircraft, thus making the most of their limited resources. Navy pilots flew Marine RF-8As, and vice versa, although the Marines had yet to change to cameras that used the larger 4.5-in format film. The Navy pilots and intelligence teams did not care for the older 70 mm format, saying it did not offer the larger, sharper, negatives of the newer film.

By this time the Navy pilots were encountering increasing amounts of flak as the photo-birds flew along the Mekong River and over the Plaine des Jars, often in bad weather mixed along with heavy anti-aircraft fire from the ground. Early on the morning of 21 May, two RF-8s launched for a road reconnaissance, and during the course of the sortie one of them was hit by ground fire and began to burn fiercely. Its pilot, Lt Charles Klusmann, managed to return to his carrier, however – his jet was again struck by flak five days later.

When the 27C-class carrier *Bon Homme Richard* sailed into the South China Sea in early May 1964, it brought with it three more RF-8As and two RA-3Bs.

Meanwhile, aboard *Bonnie Dick*'s sistership *Hancock* (CVA-19) which was also steaming west towards the action, Lt(jg) Richard Coffman (a member of the VFP-63 det embarked) was amused as he explained to a senior lieutenant commander how far north their mission would take them. The fighter pilot expressed disbelief – none of the fighter squadrons had known that the reconnaissance aircraft had gone so far into enemy territory. Coffman assured him the route was accurate and the hop fairly routine.

The pace had accelerated by mid-May, with photo pilots remaining constantly on call and often flying several missions a day. Ejection and survival procedures in this new area of operations were still in the early stages of development, and occasionally the Navy would bring an 'expert' out to lecture on how to survive in case of being shot down.

1Lt Kiely (he and John Sledge had been selected for captain by this stage) and his friends remembered one special visitor in particular – a scruffy old veteran who alighted from an A-3. The grizzled lieutenant commander had been in South-East Asia since World War 2, and he proceeded to give his young audience his impression of what they should and shouldn't do. He ended his lecture with a story about how he had once gone out into the jungle to retrieve a wounded soldier. However, a tiger had found the hapless serviceman first and was enjoying a rather gruesome meal when the lecturer arrived. Normally, when someone dies in battle, he is noted as KIA (killed in action). In this case, though, how the soldier died was not clear – before the tiger's attack, or as a result of it. So, the lieutenant commander noted, he wrote down 'EIA' for *eaten in action*!

On 2 June 1964 1Lts Carter and Kiely were scheduled as wingmen, the latter flying with Lt Cdr Bill Lott as the primary section, while Carter acted as Lt Jerry Kuechmann's number two, filling the role of 'spares' in case the primary section couldn't fly the mission.

Sure enough, as Lt Cdr Lott tried to tank from one of the A-4s, his RF-8 lost its generator and he had to return to the ship. By this stage 1Lt Kuechmann was already 'riding' his jet down on an elevator into the hangar bay, leaving 1Lt Carter up on the flight deck aft of the catapults.

The squadron immediately launched Carter to join up with 1Lt Kiely who, years later, remarked, 'Now there were two dumb lieutenants in the air – the stage was set'. The two young Marine photo pilots quickly set off on their mission before anyone could recall them. Besides, their radios had suddenly 'broken', and they couldn't have heard a recall anyway.

Heading over the Mekong River in the direction of for the Plaine des Jars (they could see Da Nang to the south), they knew they were forbidden to cross into North Vietnam to avoid antagonising the already skittish North Vietnamese. Taking advantage of breaks in the ever-present cloud layers, they spotted checkpoints that would hopefully lead them north to their target – a newly-constructed airstrip.

The two Crusaders were already encountering flak, but the black puffs were between them, with Kiely in the lead and Carter in loose trail. Kiely dutifully noted the guns' location on his knee-board for future reference as they descended below the base of the cloud deck at 2000 ft.

'By dumb luck', he said, 'we were almost on our first target. We used what we'd been taught – 500-550 knots, all cameras ready. The initial run took care of the low obliques, and a quick high-G turn brought us back for a repeat on the other side, all topped off with a very low forward-fire of some of the bulldozers and other ground equipment'.

Continuing up the road to a small village, the two Marines again picked up tracer fire, but they were going much too fast for the gunners to aim accurately – its high speed was, after all, the RF-8's only defence. Reaching the northern end of the plain, they photographed another airfield and two columns of military vehicles, which, according to the flags on the trucks, apparently belonged to the Pathet Lao.

'We took their pictures and scared the hell out of them', Kiely recalled, 'then turned back north-west for higher ground and another airfield target.'

They spotted an aircraft making an approach, and headed toward the field. At first the Marines thought the silver transport was a Soviet-built AN-8 'Camp' twin-engined turboprop. However, inspection of their photos later showed the aircraft to be an Air America C-123 Air America was the in-country 'airline' of the Central Intelligence Agency, which meandered around the hinterlands of South-East Asia throughout the war.

Nearing the end of their mission, the Marines checked their fuel. Kiely's aircraft (BuNo 146838) had been written up by another pilot for problems with its fuel-registering system, which effectively meant that he had no way of clearly monitoring his fuel flow, except to watch for a warning light on his panel. When this illuminated, it would indicate that Kiely's jet was down to 2500 lbs of fuel in the wing tanks.

Reaching 'bingo fuel' first, Kiely knew it was time to head home, but he was not prepared for a sharp drop of 1200 lbs on his main gauge. What was happening? This would leave him with just 300 lbs of fuel when they arrived at the ship – no cushion at all. Of course, this was all conjecture because of the malfunctioning gauge on the wing tanks, and he had to decided whether to keep heading for the carrier or divert to Da Nang. The latter choice was the least desirable because of the red tape in getting clearance to leave. There was also the mission requirement to get their pictures from this sortie back to the ship.

Calling the carrier to get a tanker airborne, the RF-8 pilots headed back over the water. They finally spotted a speck in the distance – *Kitty Hawk* – which radioed it was ready to recover them, and that there was an A-3 tanker standing by if needed.

With only an estimated 700 lbs of fuel left on board, Kiely took the first shot at landing.

'Calling the ball with 500 lbs showing, man, but that thing floated! I was way back on power, trying to get on speed. In close, I looked OK, but was still fighting a tendency to float.'

But his aircraft hit the deck hard, skipping all four arresting cables, and Kiely found himself bouncing back into the air. Now fuel was critical. He needed that A-3, *now.*

The tanker was right there, and although the ship called for another pass, Kiely knew his priorities and plugged in. The A-3 crew then left for an 'important' mission ashore. It was only after Kiely's saviour returned and suffered a hard landing that the truth came out – the A-3 began leaking *scotch* from one of its camera bays.

'Those jerks would have rather seen me take a dunking than hold up the booze run', he declared.

The young Marine aviators were brought down to the hangar on elevators, their jets' engines still turning. Although the air wing commander required an explanation as to why Kiely ignored the air boss's instruction to make a second pass, he was eventually satisfied, and the pilots went to see the intelligence officers who would debrief them.

The most important bit of information gleaned from the sortie was the placement of radar-controlled guns, which the intel officers did not believe. Of course, the pilots knew what they had seen. Some time later, they were called down to the photo-interpreter spaces, where they found the CarDiv Seven commander, Rear Adm William 'Bush' Bringle, and a variety of officers pouring over their photos, including the 70 mm film which, as mentioned earlier, was not considered to be of very good quality by the Navy.

It turned out that the two Marines had obtained first-class coverage of an important area, and they beamed as the admiral complimented them in front of everyone. Their forward-fire film was also good, and all things told, it was a stellar performance.

Capt Draayer, the det OINC, crowed, 'This was the masterpiece! The first flight to come back with some great photo work. When the Navy air wing commander heard two Marine lieutenants had been launched, he was fit to be tied, but I told him they could handle it'.

On 6 June Lt Klusmann's aircraft (BuNo 146823) was again hit by anti-aircraft fire, but this time the damage was too severe for a safe return, and Klusmann ejected from his RF-8A, becoming the first individual to make a combat ejection from a Crusader. This aircraft was also the first of 20 photo-Crusaders lost to enemy action, although none fell victim to MiGs.

In this early stage of the conflict, there were many areas of operational concern for the photo pilots, including survival techniques and the lack of armed escorts that could shoot back and protect the unarmed RF-8s. At this early stage in the conflict two photo-Crusaders would usually perform a mission, with one being the designated escort – primarily to look

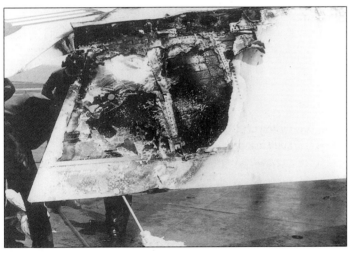

out for flak – and the second being the mission leader and picture-taker.

'Initially', Klusmann later said, 'we didn't know that everything was being planned and approved in Washington. We also didn't know how little Washington planners knew of how combat flights should be flown. After all, we were just learning, ourselves . . .' His words were tragically indicative of how the long war would be fought – at the expense of many US airmen.

On 6 June 1964 Lt Klusmann and his wingman, Lt Kuechmann,

**Above and right: On 21 May 1964, 'Corktip 918', with Lt Charles Klusmann aboard, was hit over Laos. The fire and blast from the 37 mm and 23 mm flak put holes in the wing and droops, allowing fuel to pour out. This was rapidly ignited by more 37 mm hits, the resulting fire burning for 20 minutes before going out as Klusmann climbed to 42,000 ft. He then recovered safely back aboard the *Kitty Hawk***

prepared for their mission as they had for several others. They launched from *Kitty Hawk* at 1030 and headed for their targets near the Plaine des Jarres. The weather was typically cloudy, with limited visibility, the former being heavy enough to hide many of the ground checkpoints they required to fly their route.

Trying to find a ground reference point free from clouds, Lt Klussman flew south and descended toward an area he knew had flat terrain along the Mekong River. For a while, he had the river in sight and again turned north, but the weather deteriorated once more, requiring the two Crusaders to drop down almost to tree-top level.

Flying toward the small town of Ban Ban, the American aviators knew they were heading toward an area known as 'Lead Valley', in reference to the heavy concentrations of flak occasionally encountered. The clouds were too thick, and once more Klusmann turned his flight toward another objective. His Crusader had valuable colour film, and he took pictures of the terrain.

Turning back to Ban Ban, the two RF-8 drivers stabilised at 1500 ft and 550 knots, and as Kuechmann flew off his right side, Klusmann headed for the town. Flak began popping up, but even with the tracers flying past him, Klusmann stuck to his run. As the Crusaders flashed past the enemy sites and broke right, Klusmann felt his aircraft shudder and yaw to the left, before straightening out. He knew he had been hit, probably by a small-calibre, perhaps 12.7 mm (.50 cal), shell.

'Almost immediately, I started losing pressure in my power-control systems, and Kuechmann, trailing some distance behind, said my left landing gear was hanging down. At this time, both power-control systems went off line, and the plane started handling erratically.'

With his jet now rolling right, and without any feeling in the controls, Klusmann knew he had to get out. He ejected at 10,000 ft and 450 knots.

As he descended, Klusmann saw a flash when his Crusader crashed in a canyon. For a moment it seemed that people were shooting at him from the ground. He hit a tree and fell the last 20 ft, twisting his right knee on landing.

Discarding his 'chute and flight gear, he tried making his way through the dense jungle. He heard Lt Kuechmann overhead, but soon his

PP 916 (BuNo 146825) was the only Det C aircraft that wasn't hit by flak during *Kitty Hawk*'s lively 1964 cruise. Luck deserted the jet the following year, however, for it was shot down by AAA on 8 September whilst serving with VFP-63 Det G aboard *Oriskany*. Its pilot, Lt(jg) R D Rudolph, was killed in the action – the det had lost Lt H S McWhorter to AAA just ten days earlier. In an uncanny twist of fate, RF-8A BuNo 146826 also failed to return from a mission over North Vietnam on 9 September 1965 whilst flying with Det D aboard *Coral Sea*, its pilot, Lt(jg) C B Goodwin, being posted Missing In Action

After three months as a PoW with the Pathet Lao, Lt Klusmann and a comrade escaped, finally making their way to rescue and safety at the Thai border. The tall, now-bearded, American stands out amid his Thai hosts and fellow escapee, Boun Me

Lt Klusmann arrives at Travis AFB to a welcoming committee of press photographers. He is escorted by Cdr Hap Hill of the AIRPAC staff

wingman had to head back to the ship. After another hour, Klusmann heard, then saw, a C-123 twin-engined cargo aircraft which he tried to signal, but to no avail. A small observation aircraft soon appeared, and although its pilot apparently spotted the downed Navy man – he rocked his wings and gunned his engine – there was little that could be done.

When the light aircraft and C-123 reappeared, the defensive fire from enemy positions intensified. By now, helicopters were en route, and although their crews made three passes amid heavy ground fire, they could not reach Klusmann. The photo pilot tried to get out of the tall grass, but he could now see troops coming toward him.

'I started to duck into some bushes, but they spotted me and came running up the hill and formed a circle around me.'

Klusmann had been captured by Laotian Communist forces and began three months of confinement. At first his captors brought the American to their camp, where they offered him food and a blanket. His leg was stiffening up, and he walked with increasing difficulty. Also, his stomach was upset.

He met a senior individual who tried to interrogate him in halting English. Klusmann straightforwardly told the Laotian that he could not answer his questions, which seemed to satisfy the questioner for the time being.

Although the Laotians gave him medicine and materials to write to his wife, he had already begun planning his escape. The Laotians tried to ease his physical distress and let him wash. Eventually, he was placed in a hut in which he would spend the next two months. His new quarters were close and unventilated, and next to the cooking area of the camp. The smell and smoke were overwhelming at times. The opportunities for escape looked slim, especially since his captors kept him under heavy guard.

During the rainy season in July, Klusmann dug down below the floor of his hut, but it proved to be too much trouble, and he was concerned about being discovered. He decided to try another time.

Sick with dysentery and under some physical pressure from the Laotians, Lt Klusmann tried getting back into sufficient shape to make a break. By August he was moved to another hut, which also housed more than 30 other prisoners, a few of whom spoke limited English. He learned that his new roommates were mostly political prisoners of the Pathet Lao. Befriending one individual, Klusmann eventually learned enough of the Lao language to talk with the others. He also began planning another escape.

Hoping to take advantage of the river near the camp, he was surprised when one of the other prisoners asked if he wanted to 'go under the wire' one day. Trying not to give himself away, Klusmann bided his time and a few days later he approached the man who had asked him if he wanted to leave.

Finally, Klusmann and five other Laotians eventually broke out around 27 August. The group broke up and made their way to a rendezvous point. But, as time went by, and one of the second group did not appear, Klusmann feared the worst. He convinced the other apprehensive escapees it was best to move on. The next day, the bedraggled group passed a farming village and even made it past a farmer working his rice paddy.

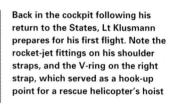

Back in the cockpit following his return to the States, Lt Klusmann prepares for his first flight. Note the rocket-jet fittings on his shoulder straps, and the V-ring on the right strap, which served as a hook-up point for a rescue helicopter's hoist

Klusmann, who had by now grown a full beard, was afraid he would stand out amongst the normally clean-shaven Laotians, so he pulled his sweater over his head.

Struggling to keep their freedom and their sense of purpose, the men tried to find food. One went into a farm house, but after three armed men appeared and dragged him away, the survivors, including Lt Klusmann, ran away.

Fighting their way over the jungle trails, encountering leeches in the streams, they finally came to a large mountain. Klusmann's companion was sure that friendly troops were on the other side. By the next afternoon, they had crossed the mountain, but now found that the leech bites were affecting them to the extent it was hard to move their legs, which they packed with mud.

The next day, in the early afternoon, the two men came to a small camp. To their great relief, the camp was indeed maintained by friendly forces and Klusmann's ordeal had come to an end. An aircraft came to pick him up.

'A fellow came running down the hill, an American, calling my name. It was the greatest sound I've ever heard in my life.'

Klusmann's experience alerted US commanders to the dangers awaiting American flight crews who parachuted into Communist captivity. How a US aviator should conduct himself under extreme mental and physical torture became an important, though largely unsolvable, problem throughout the long war in Vietnam. His three-month internment barely hinted at the horrible times in store for his fellow aviators.

Several developments came out of Charles Klusmann's debriefings,

Lt Klusmann signs for a jet after returning from Laos. Details on his flight gear include: a rescue light on his right shoulder; the rocket-jet fittings on his shoulder straps and the V-ring helo hoist connection; the chest-mounted strap that could be pulled to tighten the fit of his survival vest; and the unprotected pens on his left sleeve. Although this was the style for many years, and all aviators carried their writing implements like this, the pens constituted a major FOD hazard, and eventually, by the 1980s, a flap was sewn – usually at the squadron level – over the pen pocket to keep them from falling out in the cockpit

including the well-known survival radio, the PRC. Until this point, the crews only carried beepers, but couldn't talk to other pilots in the air. Aviator flight boots were also changed after Klusmann reported difficulty with traction in the jungle mud. The boots' soles were given grooves and a canvas top. Although, he reported his khaki flightsuit afforded better camouflage than the usual orange suits, it still was not completely satisfactory. Jungle-green suits eventually appeared, and until the advent of today's desert-coloured suits – which, after all, now reflect the current main theatre of operations – in 1990, the green flightsuits had been worn almost exclusively by all naval aviators from the mid-1960s.

After several months of recuperation, Lt Klusmann requested another tour to Vietnam, which by then had evolved into a full-blown war. However, his repeated requests were denied.

'I returned so early in the war', he says, 'that most people hadn't even started going over there.'

On the same day that Klusmann was shot down, Washington ordered another recon mission to include two RF-8s and eight fighter escorts which would be armed and authorised to deal with the increasing danger of flak and ground fire. The following day, a single RF-8A from *Constellation*'s photo det, with four F-8Ds from *Kitty Hawk*'s VF-111, overflew the Plaine des Jars. Ground fire was heavy, and the F-8Ds delivered their ordnance.

A second mission into central Laos the same day included one RF-8A and three escorts. Unfortunately, Cdr Doyle W Lynn's fighter was hit by heavy flak, and he ejected. A massive rescue effort was immediately launched and he was recovered the next day. With Chuck Klusmann's whereabouts unknown, and perhaps sensitive about not retrieving the photo pilot, the task force mounted a large search-and-rescue (SAR) effort for Cdr Lynn. Although the fighter skipper was returned, it was difficult to ignore just how hard it was going to be to both defend unarmed reconnaissance flights and rescue downed airmen in the jungles teaming with Communist troops.

The surprise series of engagements during the first week of August, collectively known as the Gulf of Tonkin Incidents, catapulted American forces directly into what had largely been a civil war between North and South Vietnam up to that point. South Vietnam and the United States had seen their respective presidents assassinated within three weeks of each other during the previous November, and although the new Lyndon Johnson administration was now beginning to focus on the unravelling situation in South-East Asia, it was ill-equipped from a psychological standpoint to cope with another major conflict in Asia – just 11 years had passed since the cease-fire in Korea. Thus, when North Vietnamese PT boats darted from their bases to make night

Marine aviators of the VMCJ-1 det aboard USS *Bon Homme Richard* in late 1964 are seen wearing various items of flight clothing, including the traditional (and highly prized) brown-leather flight jacket. The young pilot sitting on the left is engrossed in the latest 'technical' manual – a copy of *Playboy* magazine, which enjoyed a large following throughout the US military services during the war

attacks on patrolling American destroyers, the Americans found themselves sending a sporadic series of reaction raids against enemy installations, while at the same time trying to keep track of the uncontrolled flow of men and supplies into Laos and South Vietnam from the north.

In December a programme of armed reconnaissance and strike missions – codenamed *Barrel Roll* – began against specific Communist facilities along various road networks. The first *Barrel Roll* mission was flown on 17 December by four A-1 Skyraiders and four F-4s, followed by two RF-8As, all from Air Wing 9 aboard USS *Ranger* (CVA-61). Initially, the *Barrel Roll* missions yielded little, but the programme continued into 1965, and eventually began uncovering the extent of the massive Communist supply operation along the incredible network of trails and roads called the Ho Chi Minh Trail.

The Crusader's role during this early period of Vietnam combat was, primarily, one of reconnaissance. Fighters flew as escorts, and occasionally delivered Zuni rockets against selected ground targets, but it was the RF-8As of the various VFP-63 detachments, along with Marine RF-8s of VMCJ-1, that performed the greatest service.

VMCJ-1 had been alerted several times earlier in the year to be ready to deploy to South-East Asia on eight hours notice, and had already supplemented the Navy squadrons on several carriers before the August engagements. After the Gulf of Tonkin Incident, the squadron sent two RF-8As and 15 men to the *Constellation* by way of Japan and the Philippines, and when *Connie* left the war zone, its Marine reconnaissance det transferred to the *Bon Homme Richard*.

During one particular photo mission flown by the unit, Capt Lloyd Draayer (who had been the OINC of the VMCJ-1 det on board *Kitty Hawk* in June) overflew an enemy gun emplacement. One of the Navy pilots who had been escorting him had been shot down, and Capt Draayer 'buzzed' the crash site to see if the Navy pilot was alright. Although the latter was eventually recovered, Capt Draayer received a 'royal dressing down' for endangering his photographs once back aboard ship.

A second detachment relieved the *Connie/Bonnie Dick* det on 29 September, the newcomers receiving their indoctrination to shipboard

**Embarked VMCJ-1 Marines line up in front of their aircraft during the busy 1964 deployment in the *Bon Homme Richard*. Although the jet providing the immediate backdrop for this shot (BuNo 146888) survived the emergency det on CVA-31 (and CVA-64 before that), it was lost back in the USA just weeks after returning to VMCJ-1's MCAS Cherry Point home base when it crashed on 11 December 1964**

life from their Navy hosts in VF-194. The four plane captains in the second det had no experience on the Crusader, having only worked on the squadron's ancient EF-10Bs – the ELINT-version of the Korean War-vintage Douglas F3D Skyknight. However, the youngsters were quickly cross-trained on the RF-8As.

The Marines found life aboard the World War 2-era carriers less than ideal. A lack of air-conditioning, and water restrictions, made the close atmosphere a test of endurance for everyone. However, the three VMCJ-1 dets provided a measure of relief for the hard-pressed Navy photo dets. And, even when there were not enough Marine aviators, the Navy 'borrowed' their 'Leatherneck' cousins' aircraft.

Richard A Bishop was one of the plane captains in the second det aboard the *Bon Homme Richard*;

'I think we all experienced a certain amount of apprehension that was compounded by the fact that we did not have the luxury of time to become oriented. One night we were drinking beer in a bar in Olongapo, and, less than 24 hours later, we were actively involved in combat operations. We stumbled through our first couple of launches and recoveries by watching and talking to the Navy plane captains.

'It did not take us long to find out that combat operations on the flight deck of a carrier can be hot, tiring, dirty, long and dangerous. On a typical day, we would launch and recover aircraft four or five times. The flight deck crews seldom got to sleep past 0500. By the time we recovered the last flight, serviced the aircraft, spotted them for the next morning's launch, it was 2200. This went on seven days a week.

'During flight operations, we were required to have two plane captains on each aircraft at all times. We had to pre-flight the aircraft, service any systems requiring attention, secure the aircraft with two tie-down chains per landing gear during the day – three at night – and ride the brakes during spotting, or positioning, the plane. Since someone had to be with the aircraft all the time, we had to eat and perform our personal chores in shifts.

'The only stage that we really had any free time was when our aircraft were out on a mission – maybe 1 1/2 to 2 hours. Some of the guys would find a shop or office where they could just sit and drink coffee. A lot of

Four light-photo dets are represented in this 1965 photograph taken aboard the *Coral Sea*. VMCJ-1's Det Bravo helped the VFP-63 dets, supplying jets and pilots to fly the large number of missions required during this early stage of the war. Representatives of VF-111, flying F-8Ds, are also shown on the far right

RF-8A BuNo 146866 of VMCJ-1 in mid-1964. It was probably assigned to either the det aboard the *Kitty Hawk* or the *Hancock*. Later converted into an RF-8G, this jet was lost in an operational accident in the USA whilst serving with VFP-63 on 31 July 1970

VFP-63 Det L's Lt(jg) Richard Coffman finishes some post-mission paperwork in the intel spaces of the *Hancock* during the carrier's 1964-65 TF 77 deployment – the first of a record eight combat cruises to Vietnam. Photo pilots divided their time between the intelligence department, other duties within the squadron and, of course, flying. Pre-flight planning, briefing and post-mission debriefs often took place in the small spaces of the intel department

time was spent talking with a friend and watching the water go by. Every once in a while, one of the destroyers escorting us would stop in the water and let their crews swim off the side of the ship, lowering nets to close off a small section in case there were sharks around.

'I think launching the aircraft – at least for the first few times – scared me more than any other operation aboard the carrier. With all the aircraft turning up, you couldn't hear anything. If you saw someone walk directly in front of an intake, or about to walk into the exhaust blast of an aircraft, you couldn't yell a warning. All you could do was watch. This became especially true as we got more tired and became lax in observing safety precautions.

'I would like to think I may have saved a sailor's life while we were launching aircraft one afternoon. The aircraft to the left of my plane pulled out and made a left turn onto the catapult. I saw what was about to happen and knew I was going to be hit by the full exhaust blast. I ducked down under my plane's nose and straddled one of the tie-down chains. With my back to the turning aircraft, I grabbed the chain between my legs and held on for dear life. I looked up and noticed a sailor standing on the flight deck in front of my aircraft. He had not seen the turning plane and caught the full blast and was thrown toward the side of the ship. As he flew by, I managed to reach out and grab his shirt while still holding the chain with my other hand.

'Recovery could also get a little hairy. Once the aircraft landed, the pilots would fold the wings and taxy up to the bow. The planes would be chocked, chained, and the engines shut down. Once the recovery was completed, we would immediately start refuelling, refilling oxygen bottles, and hanging bombs and rockets for the next launch, all at the same time – something you would never do during peacetime. One spark or drop of fuel in combination with liquid oxygen could have blown us all away.'

Bishop's det transferred to the *Ticonderoga* on 9 October, with VF-53 as their hosts. They moved to the *Constellation* 20 days later, where they were attached to Carrier Air Group 14, before eventually being relieved by a new VMCJ-1 det on 10 November.

# 1965-68 – MISSIONS AND LOSSES MOUNT

Throughout the Vietnam War, the only constant air operation was that of reconnaissance. Whether there was a bombing halt (the bane and frustration of every aircrew from every tactical community) or no matter if the terrible weather patterns of South-East Asia closed everything else down, the reconnaissance flights launched.

The Air Force had its dedicated photo community, which flew a variety of aircraft including RF-101A/Hs and RF-4Cs, whilst the Navy and Marine Corps, in turn, operated RA-3Bs, RA-5Cs RF-4Bs and, of course, the RF-8, which came in two models – the RF-8A and RF-8G.

Three squadrons flew reconnaissance Crusaders in Vietnam – the Navy's VFP-62 and -63 and the Marine Corps' VMCJ-1. By 1968 only VFP-63 was still flying RF-8Gs, for VFP-62 had decommissioned in January 1968 after just one deployment to Vietnam, whilst VMCJ-1 had

**The 27C-class *Essex* carrier *Hancock* replenishes at sea. This ability to 'gas-and-go' on the run was vital to the Seventh Fleet's programme of maintaining long line periods up and down the long coast of the two Vietnams throughout the war, and amounted to the same importance as the in-flight refuelling capability of aircraft. The flight deck is crowded with F-8s, A-4s and an E-1B of CVW-21**

A bow-on view of the *Bonnie Dick* in early 1968. Until its retirement after a combat cruise in 1970, the *Bon Homme Richard* was one of the busiest of the 27C carriers. Its 1967 cruise produced nearly half of the MiG kills attributed to the Crusader (eight were shared between VF-24 and -211)), but also resulted in the embarked air wing suffering one of the highest loss rates of the first half of the war (21 aircraft were lost in action, and a further two operationally)

An RF-8G of VFP-62 receives pre-launch attention. Its in-flight refuelling probe is extended for checking, and one of the photomates (PHs) prepares to close a camera-bay door. Note the *EYES OF THE FLEET* marking on the wing bulkhead – this motto traded back and forth between VFP-62, whose nickname was actually 'Fightin' Photo', and VFP-63

begun changing its RF-8As for RF-4Bs in October 1966 – as an aside, a VMCJ-1 RF-8A pilot was credited with a truck kill when he roared fast and low over a Communist vehicle on a mountain trail, causing the startled occupant to drive straight off a cliff.

While VFP-62 basked in its moment of glory in 1962 during the Cuban Missile Crisis, VFP-63 sent its detachments to the Pacific carriers without much publicity. Like its Atlantic Fleet sister squadron, VFP-63 had evolved from several different reconnaissance units, some of which had seen considerable combat in World War 2 and the Korean War. VFP-63 was redesignated in 1961, and became the longest-serving squadron in Vietnam, covering every major action over every country in South-East Asia. Its pilots were among the most highly decorated of any service in the war, yet few photo pilots made it into the higher echelons of naval rank. This lack of professional progress was odd, considering how much responsibility a junior RF-8 pilot shouldered.

For instance, a lieutenant (junior grade) planned and led a mission, even though his escort crew might include more senior aviators – even the commanding officer of the fighter squadron. It called for diplomacy, tact and experience, and maturity at a young age. Of course, things did not always go smoothly, but for the most part, and especially as the war progressed and fighter squadrons accepted the requirement for the photo pilots to be the flight leaders, the 'unarmed and unafraid' members – most of whom would seriously dispute the 'unafraid' portion of their motto – of the VFP detachments established themselves in any carrier air wing.

One development that occurred in October 1965 was delivery to VFP-63 of the first RF-8G, with the first deployment in USS *Coral Sea* (CVA-43) taking place in mid-1966. The 'Golf' was a rebuilt RF-8A, and sported new additions such as the distinctive ventral fins, which had first appeared on the F-8C and added stability at high speed, an uprated engine in the Pratt & Whitney J-57-P-22, offering 16,000 lbs static thrust, hard-harness electrical wiring (*text continues on page 49*)

*FDR* with its air wing. One of three ships in the so-called 'battle-carrier' class, it was the first of the trio to retire, after carrying new Marine Corps AV-8A Harriers on their first deployment in 1974. Its sister-ships – *Midway* and *Coral Sea* – remained in fleet service for another 15 years, with *Midway* seeing extensive action during *Desert Storm* in 1991

Det Lima RF-8A BuNo 146830 descends with its hook extended in preparation for its approach to *Hancock*. This aircraft earned the unenviable distinction of being the last A-model lost in action on 21 June 1966 when it was shot down by AAA whilst on a sortie from CVA-19. Its pilot, Lt L L Eastman, was quickly captured by the North Vietnamese. He was the second Det Lima pilot to become a PoW during the deployment, Lt J Heilig having been captured on 5 May 1966 after his jet (BuNo 146831) was struck by AAA. These were not the only losses suffered by the det during this particularly bloody deployment, however, for Lt T Walster had been shot down and killed on 9 April in BuNo 144611

A view of an RF-8G cockpit. The handle of the control column is typical, with many different buttons and wheels to control systems and surfaces. The large, circular window atop the main panel is the pilot's viewfinder, which looks out directly beneath the aircraft's nose along its flight path. The black-and-white globe immediately beneath it is the horizontal-situation indicator (HSI), similar to an artificial horizon. The assortment of toggle switches and knobs is apparent

# COLOUR PLATES

This colour section profiles the RF-8s flown by the US Navy and Marine Corps light reconnaissance units involved in the Cuban Crisis and the conflict in South-East Asia. All the artwork has been specially commissioned for this volume, and profile artist Tom Tullis and figure artist Mike Chappell have gone to great pains to illustrate the aircraft, and their pilots, as accurately as possible following exhaustive research by the author. None of the photo-Crusaders depicted on the following pages have been illustrated in colour artwork before, and the schemes shown have been fully authenticated either by the pilot(s) who flew the aircraft in combat, or from contemporary official images taken by US Navy and Marine Corps photographers or naval aviators serving during the periods in question.

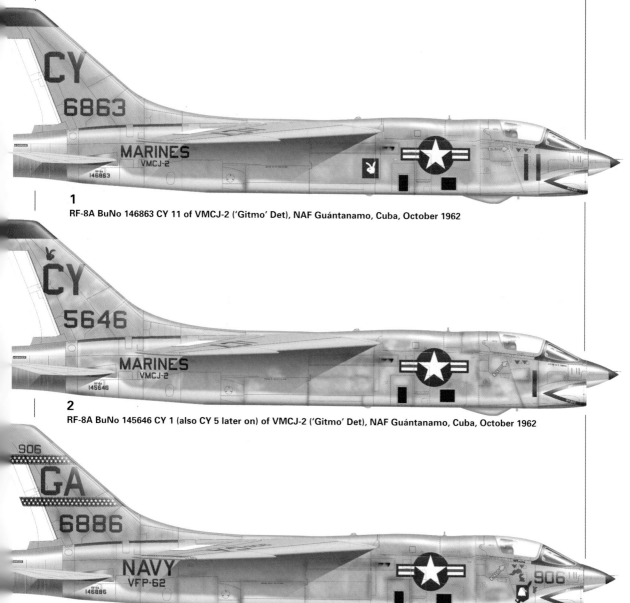

**1**
RF-8A BuNo 146863 CY 11 of VMCJ-2 ('Gitmo' Det), NAF Guántanamo, Cuba, October 1962

**2**
RF-8A BuNo 145646 CY 1 (also CY 5 later on) of VMCJ-2 ('Gitmo' Det), NAF Guántanamo, Cuba, October 1962

**3**
RF-8A BuNo 146886 GA 906 of VFP-62, NAS Key West, November 1962

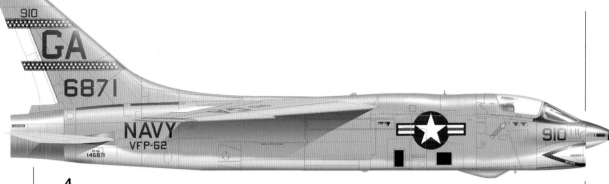

**4**
RF-8A BuNo 146871 GA 910 flown by Cdr William Ecker, CO of VFP-62, NAS Key West, late November 1962

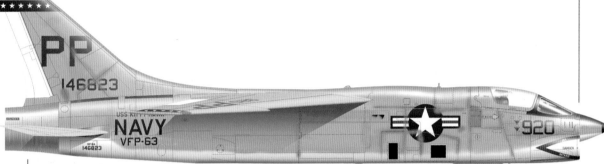

**5**
RF-8A BuNo 146823 PP 920 flown by Lt Charles Klusmann, VFP-63 Det C, USS *Kitty Hawk*, June 1964

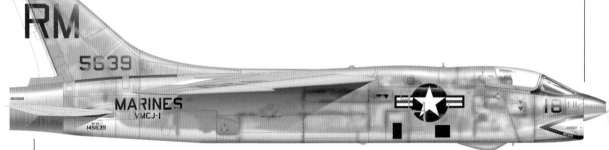

**6**
RF-8A BuNo 145639 RM 18 of VMCJ-1 aboard USS *Kitty Hawk*, May/June 1964

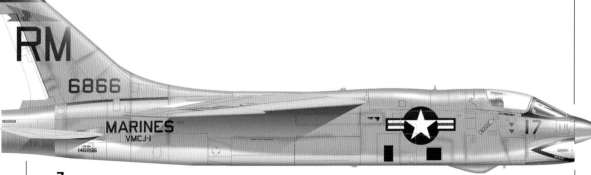

**7**
RF-8A BuNo 146866 RM 17 flown by 1Lt Denis Kiely of VMCJ-1 aboard USS *Kitty Hawk*, May/June 1964

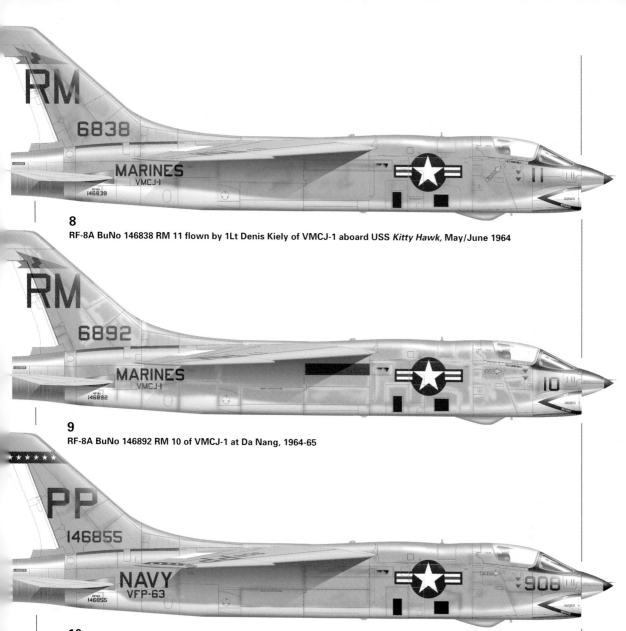

**8**
RF-8A BuNo 146838 RM 11 flown by 1Lt Denis Kiely of VMCJ-1 aboard USS *Kitty Hawk,* May/June 1964

**9**
RF-8A BuNo 146892 RM 10 of VMCJ-1 at Da Nang, 1964-65

**10**
RF-8A BuNo 146855 PP 908 of VFP-63 Det F aboard USS *Constellation*, 1964

**11**
RF-8A BuNo 145632 PP 967 of VFP-63 Det A aboard USS *Midway*, 1965

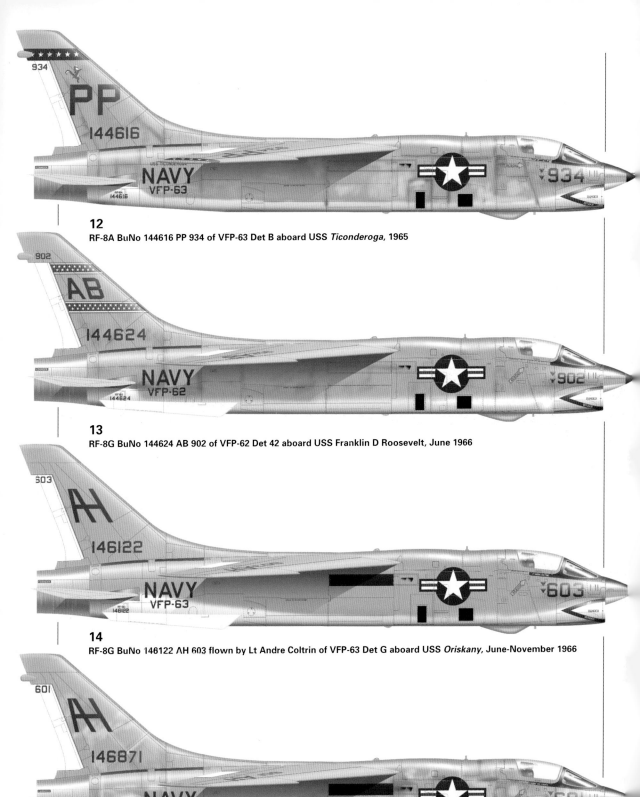

**12**
RF-8A BuNo 144616 PP 934 of VFP-63 Det B aboard USS *Ticonderoga*, 1965

**13**
RF-8G BuNo 144624 AB 902 of VFP-62 Det 42 aboard USS Franklin D Roosevelt, June 1966

**14**
RF-8G BuNo 146122 AH 603 flown by Lt Andre Coltrin of VFP-63 Det G aboard USS *Oriskany*, June-November 1966

**15**
RF-8G BuNo 146871 AH 601 of VFP-63 Det G aboard USS *Oriskany*, June-November 1966

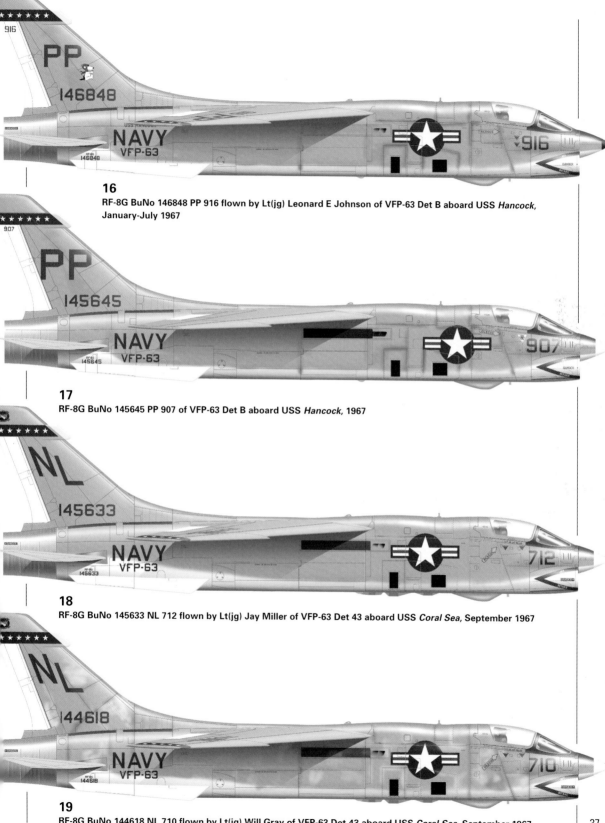

**16**
RF-8G BuNo 146848 PP 916 flown by Lt(jg) Leonard E Johnson of VFP-63 Det B aboard USS *Hancock*, January-July 1967

**17**
RF-8G BuNo 145645 PP 907 of VFP-63 Det B aboard USS *Hancock*, 1967

**18**
RF-8G BuNo 145633 NL 712 flown by Lt(jg) Jay Miller of VFP-63 Det 43 aboard USS *Coral Sea*, September 1967

**19**
RF-8G BuNo 144618 NL 710 flown by Lt(jg) Will Gray of VFP-63 Det 43 aboard USS *Coral Sea*, September 1967

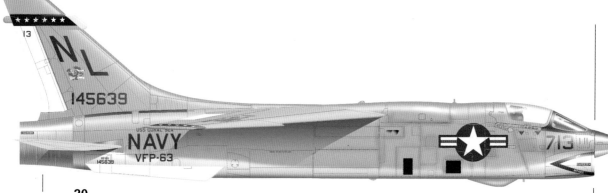

**20**
RF-8G BuNo 145639 NL 713 of VFP-63 Det 43 aboard USS *Coral Sea*, 1968

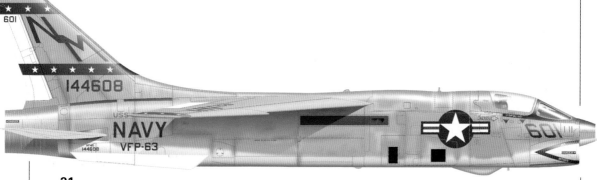

**21**
RF-8G BuNo 145636 NM 603 of VFP-63 Det 4 aboard USS *Oriskany*, 1971

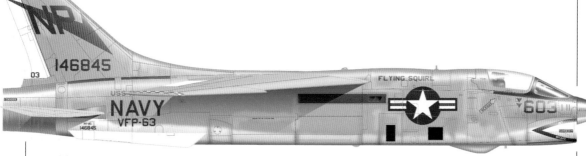

**22**
RF-8G BuNo 146845 NP 603 of VFP-63 Det 1 aboard USS *Hancock*, 1971

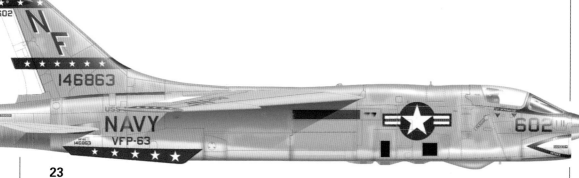

**23**
RF-8G BuNo 146863 NF 602 flown by Capt Jim Morgan, USAF, of VFP-63 Det 3 aboard USS *Midway*, 1971

**24**
RF-8G BuNo 146892 NP 612 of VFP-63 Det 1 aboard USS *Hancock*, 1972

**25**
RF-8G BuNo 146876 PP 901 of Cdr J M Schulze, Commander of VFP-63, NAS Miramar, 1972

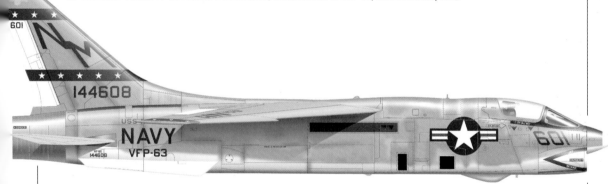

**26**
RF-8G BuNo 144608 NM 601 of VFP-63 Det 4 aboard USS *Oriskany*, June 1972 to January 1973

**27**
RF-8G BuNo 146856 NF 601 flown by Lt Cdr Will Gray, OINC of VFP-63's Det 3 aboard USS *Midway* in December 1973

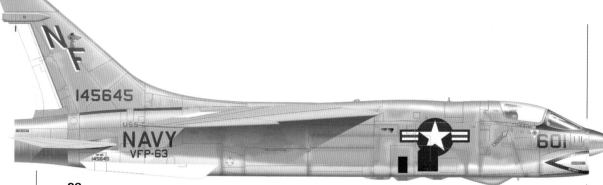

**28**
RF-8G BuNo 145645 NF 601 flown by Lt Cdr Will Gray of VFP-63 Det 3 aboard USS *Midway*, 1974

**29**
RF-8G BuNo 146835 NL 603 of VFP-63 Det 5 aboard USS *Coral Sea*, 1974

**1**
Cdr William Ecker, CO of
VFP-62 during the Cuban
missile crisis in October/
November 1962

**2**
Capt Harold 'Hoss' Austin of
VMCJ-2's 'Gitmo Det',
Guántanamo Bay, Cuba,
October/November 1962

**3**
Capt John I Hudson of VMCJ-2,
temporarily assigned to VFP-62
during the Cuban missile crisis of
October/November 1962

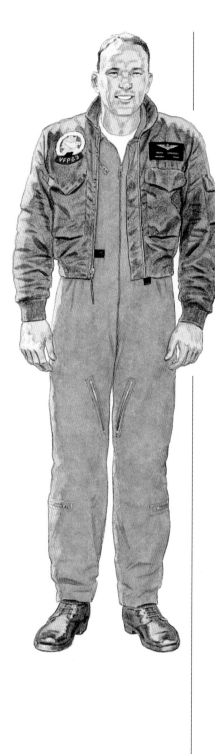

**4**
Lt Charles Klusmann of VFP-63,
NAS Miramar, early 1965

**5**
Lt Cdr J M Schulze, OINC VFP-63
Det B aboard USS *Hancock*, South
China Sea, 1967

**6**
Lt Cdr Tom Tucker, OINC VFP-63
Det G, NAS Miramar, early 1966

**1**

**2**

**3**

**4**

5

6

7

8

9

10

11

12

13

14

15

16

17A

17B

17C

17D

and various upgraded avionics. Better ECM (electronic counter-measures) gear was installed, and the RF-8A's cameras were also changed in the G-model – an improved panoramic camera replaced the trimetro-gen equipment. The new sensor, the KA-66, and the later KA-68, were true panoramic cameras, sweeping from horizon to horizon instead of the earlier model that involved three separate prisms.

A total of 73 RF-8As was remanufactured as RF-8Gs, from the 144 original F8U-1P (RF-8A) photo-Crusaders manufactured between 1956 and 1960. By late 1966, the 'Golf' had completely replaced the 'Alpha' in Navy dets, although the Marines were still flying the earlier model from shore bases.

## THE AIs AND PIs

One important aspect of the RF-8's mission was the close working relationship between the pilots and their ground team – especially the small group of specialists who looked at the mission film. Besides its complement of pilots and normal maintenance and administrative personnel, each det included four or five specially trained individuals. These enlisted men and officers planned, briefed, debriefed and reported the flights of their RF-8 pilots, showing a close involvement with the overall mission not found in other squadrons.

The enlisted men were Photographic Intelligencemen (PIs), a rate established in 1957, while the junior officers who accompanied the det in the intelligence departments were designated Photographic Interpreters (PIs). Photographer's Mates (PHs) maintained the aircraft camera systems and worked closely with the PTs and PIs. These specialists were a vital part of the overall mission, and they assumed responsibilities out of proportion to their relatively junior years – to further confuse things, PTs were redesignated Intelligence Specialists (ISs) in 1974.

Lt (later Capt) Louis R Mortimer served two 11-month cruises in Vietnam, one in the *Coral Sea* and one in the *Ticonderoga*. He had enlisted in the Naval Reserve at 17, and maintained his affiliation while going through college. Following his commissioning in 1966 through the Aviation Officer Candidate School (AOCS) – of *An Officer and a Gentleman* fame – he received orders to attend the joint service school for intelligence officers at Lowrey Air Force Base, near Denver, Colorado. During this intensive six-month course, he was taught various disciplines, including basic photo interpretation, weaponeering (which instructed the requirements specific targets dictated when choosing the proper ordnance for their destruction) and briefing techniques;

'I always laugh when I think how I got to light photo. I got low grades in photo interpretation. Two of us wanted the VFPs. The other man went to heavy photo (VAP) – the A-3 units on Guam.

'Originally, I thought I was best suited to a fighter squadron, but they told me they want a more mature, sophisticated individual to work with the photo pilots and shoulder greater responsibility. I didn't know how true that was, but later I thought you did need that maturity.

'After Lowrey, we went to a three-week school at FITCPAC – Fleet Intelligence Training Center, Pacific – in Alameda, near San Francisco. This course gave us attack-intelligence training for carrier operations as carried out by CTF 77 (the main component of the on-going carrier

Then-Lt Cdr Lou Mortimer checks mission film in 1977. At this time he was the air intelligence officer for reserve-manned VFP-306. Mortimer had earlier served two long 11-month tours aboard two carriers in Vietnam, working through the pivotal 1968 Tet Offensive during which his *Coral Sea* det of RF-8Gs worked overtime keeping track of the flood of enemy trucks and supplies heading south. He retired as a senior captain after a long career and several unit commands

presence in the South China Sea, on *Yankee* and *Dixie* Stations), rules of engagement and South-East Asian geography, culture and history.

'Then they sent me to San Diego to VFP-63. I checked in at night. The first guy I met was Jay Miller, who was going through the RF-8 training syllabus. I signed in with the duty officer, and in came Jay, fresh from a flight.

'"Christ, I really scared myself. This night flying's for the birds. Hi, I'm Jay Miller", and he stuck out his hand. I came back the next morning for an interview with the CO of the squadron. He introduced me to the department heads. Then I learned the difference between an Air Intelligence Officer (AIO) and Photo Interpretation Officer (PIO). The AIO never went to sea. I would be the junior PIO for my det and would go almost immediately to Vietnam aboard the *Coral Sea*.

'We learned the RF-8's camera system with the pilots. They flew the mission, and we PIOs graded their film. So, we were teamed very early with the junior pilots. We spent six months at Miramar learning the cameras before going to sea.

'We formed the det early and integrated with CVW-15 to go to work-ups in Fallon, Nevada. Boy! It was cold up there! Interestingly enough, the film was processed right at Fallon, contrary to the situation after the war when all photo-mission film went to San Diego. That's when I learned how important it was to have a good working relationship with the people in the photo lab. They could make or break you many times over. You had to be firm, but *enlightened*, humane. If you screwed with the photomates, your whole mission could be destroyed – everything a pilot risked his life for.'

Mortimer worked through an intense period of combat operations, learning his job, and working with the many individuals in his det, and in the air wing. He also went through the turmoil of experiencing the loss of his OINC shortly after the *Coral Sea* arrived on the line;

'Lt Cdr Jim Vescelius became our OINC. Originally, he was going to be the second in command, because he was junior. Lt Cdr Ron Sonniksen was supposed to be our OINC. But, there was a problem with the OINC of the *Oriskany* det, so Sonniksen went to that ship and Vescelius took over.

'We decided to break up the duty section to include a day and a night officer. There was so much film coming in. Naturally, as the junior guy, I got to be the night person, look at the film and write the many reports.

Lt(jg) E H Haffey (right) and PT2 J C Shokitano go through mission film from Det Bravo RF-8Gs during the Vietnam cruise aboard *Hancock* in 1967. The copy of the service paper *Stars and Stripes* on the table notes that Navy and Air Force pilots have recently shot down three MiGs. The two men are working with a portable light table, with spools at each end for film rolls. A magnifier loop and stereo viewer also sit on the light table's glass

A photomate prepares to install a camera in this RF-8G of VFP-63 at NAS Miramar in 1969. PHs were the camera mechanics, and without their knowledge and skill, the intense photo-reconnaissance effort performed throughout the war would have been impossible to sustain

Enlisted photomates retrieve exposed film from an RF-8G's camera aboard USS *Intrepid* at the completion of yet another sortie

'We had three PTs – a 2nd class petty officer, 3rd class petty officer and a striker, the latter individual being a non-rated "apprentice" PT. We had five pilots. The senior PI interacted with the Strike Ops Department, who determined which targets would be hit by the air wing. He also handled daily messages.

'Most of the time, we PIs assigned the targets to the pilots, as the flight schedule came out for the following day. Then, we would work with the pilots, briefing them on the mission requirements and enemy defences. We'd research the target, trying to find previous photos, so they'd know what it looked like. Our pilots would also listen to the briefing given by ship AIs for the whole air wing.

'One distinction was that all the other air wing pilots were debriefed by the ship AIs, but we in VFP-63 debriefed our own pilots. Debriefing was a tough act because some pilots tended to look down on the poor AI trying to get information from the pilots who had been on the mission while he was safe on the ship. But there were only a few of those types.

'Our photo pilots were always anxious to talk to us, however, because they understood the need for the information to look at their film. Photo pilots were more sophisticated than other wing pilots, because the photo pilot was the flight leader, even though he might be junior – *way* junior – in rank to his escort. Even if the escort pilot was the skipper of the fighter

51

squadron, the "jaygee" in the RF-8 was the flight lead. Sometimes it would cause friction.

'We read the mission film for bomb damage assessment (BDA) after a strike to see if another strike was needed. The air wing would hit a target, closely followed by our photo-bird. That was something we told them not to do, because the Vietnamese knew that the unarmed photo-bird would come along, fly straight and level, and they could blow him away. But they did it that way. That's how our OINC, Lt Cdr Vescelius, got bagged on 21 September 1967 during a strike over Haiphong (in RF-8G BuNo 144623). We needed immediate BDA, right after the bombs, showing the bursts, and he flew way too low in an effort to get really good coverage. He broke the 3500-ft altitude minimums.

'When we got back into port, we picked up another experienced pilot, Lt Andre Coltrin, as our OINC, to finish our first line period. Later, on our second line period, Lt Cdr Bill Rosson became our OINC. He was one of the nicest guys you'd ever want to meet.'

## DEADLY SKIES

From the first *Barrel Roll* mission in late 1964, the RF-8 pilot faced a dangerous tour whilst operating with TF 77. Before he went to the *Coral Sea*'s det in 1967, Lt Coltrin had seen considerable action with *Oriskany*'s Det G. VF-111's Dick Schaffert (whose experiences are related in the companion volume on the F-8) recalled that as an escort pilot, he had 'chased Andre across the Thanh Hoa Bridge and uptown Haiphong more times than I care to remember'.

A photomate installs camera-mount brackets in an RF-8G fuselage for the aircraft's oblique cameras. This views shows to advantage the wire bundles and fixtures associated with the large cameras, which had to withstand the shock of catapult launches and 130-mph traps on recovery

On 17 August 1966 Coltrin 'blew' across the dikes at Bac Giang on the Thuong River at only 100 ft and 675 knots. Later in the war, there would be restrictions against flying photo missions below 3500 ft within the range of most small-arms fire, but not now. Coltrin hoped to evade enemy radar at this altitude. His RF-8G (BuNo 146871) was actually growing too hot to touch.

Coltrin's mission was to photograph POL (petroleum, oil and lubricants) facilities near Kep airfield, north-east of Hanoi. Air Force exchange pilot Capt Wil Abbott of VF-111 flew escort in an F-8C – Abbott was later shot down in September, his aircraft becoming one of just three confirmed F-8s lost to North Vietnamese MiGs. He spent the next six-and-a-half years as a PoW, being repatriated in 1973.

After taking his pictures, Coltrin turned north at Bac Giang with Abbott close behind. The photo

Another view of a photomate at work, this time making a power check of the jet's cameras. Note the caution above the HSI, indicating that a zero-zero ejection seat is installed in the aircraft

*Intrepid* saw considerable action in the early part of the war, with one of her VF-111 F-8Cs making the last MiG kill officially credited to the Crusader. The old World War 2 carrier had suffered a *kamikaze* strike in 1945, forcing it to retire for major repairs before returning to the war zone just days prior to the Japanese surrender. Her reconfiguration as a 27C ship shows up well here, with the angle deck providing a landing area that would not conflict with the main launch area at the bow

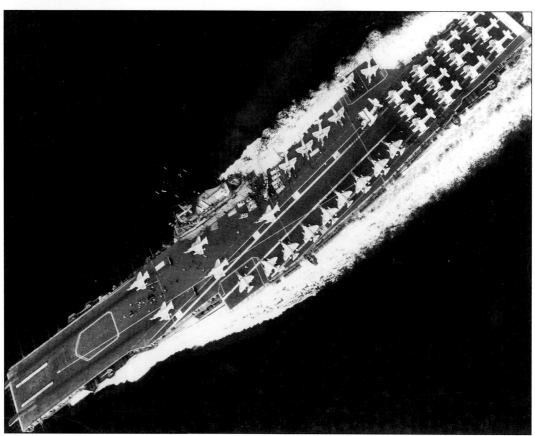

pilot saw the 1200-foot peak he would use as a checkpoint. Suddenly, the RF-8 shuddered as it took hits from flak. The sky was thick with white and black bursts with red centres. At this height, it wouldn't take much to knock him down. He flew so low that later, looking at his mission film, he could see clothes on washlines as he flew through the outskirts of Hanoi.

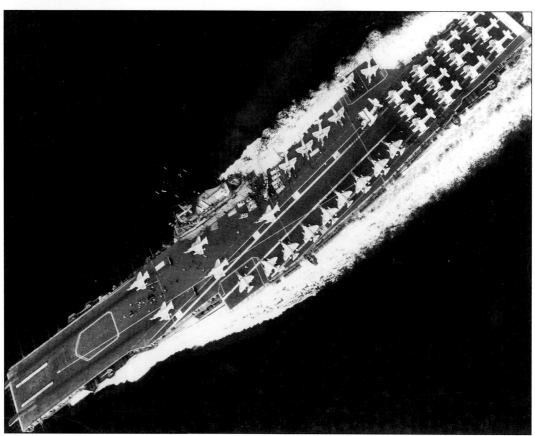

The veteran carrier *Hancock* during a 1968 combat cruise. The ship first fought in World War 2 and found herself at the spearhead during the Vietnam War. She had two bow catapults and a centrally located elevator. An A-4 rests on the lift, which was in a strategic location if the carrier sustained damage, or the elevator became stuck in the down position

RF-8G BuNo 146897 during a low-level mission over South Vietnam on 20 July 1966. The aircraft was part of Det G aboard *Oriskany* at the time this photograph was taken. Note the low visibility, with clouds hugging the ridgeline – typical conditions at various times of the year

'The snow-covered mountains I thought I had seen from a distance turned out to be 37 mm flak bursts. I felt like every gun and missile site in Vietnam had us in their sights.'

Fighting to maintain control, Coltrin watched the big, circular viewfinder on his main panel dissolve and his hydraulic and fuel gauges begin a steady decline. He called Abbott.

'Hey, I'm taking hits. We'd better get out. My hydraulics and fuel are starting to unwind.'

Abbott came back. 'Can you tell if it's just the dials?'

'We'll know in a few seconds', Coltrin replied.

Climbing back to a safer altitude, he monitored the gauges, but the stricken aircraft kept flying. Breathing a little easier, the two pilots headed toward a tiny island north of Cam Pha – the mission's exit point. But, Coltrin wondered, did he have enough fuel to make it back to *Oriskany*?

An orbiting A-4 tanker pilot was

Lt Andre Coltrin in an RF-8G during a carrier qualification period at NAS Miramar. His large white flight helmet features a dual-action knob in the centre that lowered one of two visors – clear or smoked – depending on the light. Note the cloth strap attaching the canopy to the fuselage, this simple device helping protect the canopy's hinge pins from breaking in wind gusts. The pilot also used the strap to pull the canopy down

listening to the two Crusader drivers and called to say if they could rendezvous, he would give them fuel. After some anxious moments, Lt Coltrin spotted the A-4, a buddy pack slung underneath. It took a few tries, running on his adrenaline as he was, but Coltrin was finally to hit the tanker's basket and take on enough fuel to recover back aboard. His problems were exacerbated by not having an airspeed indicator to help him match the A-4's speed. He had to rely on the tanker pilot's calls.

A post-flight check showed several flak-shell fragments in his RF-8 – one large piece had hit just inches from the main fuel manifold. Coltrin received one of his three DFCs for the mission.

The two-year period 1966-67 were undoubtedly the most 'colourful', and at times the most dangerous and tragic, for the photo-reconnaissance pilots of VFP-63. After the flurry of the combined Navy-Marine dets 18 months before, the Crusader photo detachments had re-established their respective turfs, with the Navy flying from the smaller *Essex*-class 27-Charlie ships *Oriskany*, *Hancock*, *Bon Homme Richard*, *Intrepid* and *Shangri-la* (which made only one combat cruise), and three-ship *Midway*-class, and the Marine RF-8As operating from Da Nang until 1967, when they completed transition to RF-4Bs.

The photo dets were designated by letters – E, F, G and L – until early 1967 when they took on the hull numbers of their carriers, as in Det 34 for *Oriskany*, or Det 43 for *Coral Sea*. Although the aviators of these small groups saw sustained combat throughout the nine-year war, it was during the early middle stage of the conflict that they earned both their reputations and battle scars, usually at the expense of some very good, dedicated reconnaissance pilots.

## HARBOUR RESCUE

On 30 August 1966 Andre Coltrin flew a mission in RF-8G BuNo 146874 Alpha Hotel (the air wing tail letters) 602. Less than 24 hours later, 'Corktip 602' had crashed into Haiphong Harbour, and its pilot, det OINC Lt Cdr Tom Tucker, was in the fight of his life. ('Corktip' was VFP-63's call sign until 1972, when it became 'Baby Giant').

Tucker had bailed out of his stricken jet and was now the object of interest from enemy units on the shore. The bounty on American pilots

was more than a year's pay for most of the North Vietnamese population, and any lucky fisherman who scooped up a 'Yankee Air Pirate' had it made for a while.

As the RF-8 pilot tried to keep himself pointed out to sea, Lt Cdr Foster Teague, Tucker's VF-111 escort pilot (and future F-4 MiG-killer), was organising a rescue effort. Teague, whose nickname was 'Tooter', would make his own combat ejection on 12 August 1967 from F-8C BuNo 146993 after taking hits from groundfire during a TARCAP mission. He was recovered, uninjured.

'Come now, or don't bother', Teague radioed.

Cdr Bob Vermilya, CO of SH-3A squadron HS-6 aboard USS *Kearsarge* (CVS-33), heard the call and launched with his crew. Outfitted with M-60 machine guns in the side windows, the Sea King could at least defend itself to an extent.

Arriving on scene, Vermilya couldn't see the downed pilot on his first pass. Machine gun and mortar fire came toward him, and he could see at least two SAMs launch toward Teague in his F-8E as he orbited high above. As he slowed to allow his cabin crew a more stable base from which to deploy their rescue sling, Vermilya heard his senior crewman, AWC Tom Gresham, call, 'We've got him'. The resourceful men in the cabin had lowered a cable and horse collar into the water, and Tucker had grabbed the offering.

The helo pilot immediately made a 180° turn and ran, as fast as his shuddering aircraft could go, even as the cabin crew retrieved Lt Cdr Tucker, reeling him up, soaking wet and all smiles. PH2 Mike Delamore, a Seventh Fleet photographer, snapped a series of pictures that became

**VFP-63 pilots pose in front of a fighter during a CQ in 1966. Referring to themselves as the 'Pussy Galore' flight, they had their yellow ascots suitably monogrammed with the letters 'PG' – 'Pussy Galore' was a female character in the then-current James Bond *Goldfinger* film. One half of these aviators were shot down and killed, or imprisoned, in the coming months. Andre Coltrin is at the extreme left, front row, Lt Cdr Tom Tucker, the det OINC, second from right, standing, and Lt Cdr Jim Vescelius second from right, front row. Tucker was shot down over Haiphong Harbour in August 1966 and rescued, but Vescelius was posted MIA after he was downed in September 1967. The pilot to Coltrin's left survived a crash into the LSO platform, but the remaining 12 people on the platform were killed. The aviator on Tucker's left was an air group commander who was shot down in a 'Spad'. Although he survived ditching his A-1, he was apparently shot to death as he stood on the wing of his sinking aircraft**

RF-8G BuNo 145637 had its wing-tip badly damaged by flak during a mission on 20 October 1967

Lt Coltrin traps aboard *Oriskany* in June 1966 to end yet another sortie whilst part of VFP 63 Det G. CVA-34 had only arrived in-theatre that month, and commenced its first period on the line on 30 June

In one of the war's most photographed combat sequences of the war, Lt Cdr Tom Tucker, OINC of Det G aboard *Oriskany*, rides the hoist up to the SH-3A from HS-6 during a frantic SAR over Haiphong Harbour on 31 August 1966. The daring rescue was made under intense fire from North Vietnamese positions, and underscored the lengths to which all US SAR crews would go to rescue downed airmen

one of the best known examples of an actual mission in Vietnam. The HS-6 crew delivered the soggy, but happy, photo pilot back to his carrier, then returned to *Kearsarge*. Although he had hurt his back, Tucker had not been in too much pain to man an M-60 and fire back at his tormentors as the SH-3 left enemy territory. Tucker later commanded VF-51 – one of several Crusader drivers who 'cross-pollinated' from the photo to fighter community, or vice versa. He led his squadron in transitioning from the F-8E to F-4B.

Lt(jg) Leonard Johnson was a young, eager, newcomer to *Hancock*'s Det Lima in the spring of 1966;

'Our unit suffered the highest loss rate. When I told other aviators I was in VFP-63, their reaction was like saying, "You poor SOB!" It was as if you told them you had cancer. Det Lima lost its first pilot in April 1966. Lt(jg) Tom Waltser was hit over Vinh (in RF-8G BuNo 144611). The

damage precluded a safe landing, so he ejected off Da Nang. But his flotation gear didn't inflate for some reason, and he was dragged below the surface.

'A rescue diver jumped in and grabbed his 'chute. He hung on as long

as he could, but Tom's gear was filling with water and the diver had to let go to keep from being pulled down, too.

'The first two replacement pilots assigned to the det turned in their wings. Another developed stomach problems and kept cancelling his training flights.

'Although I hadn't finished my training, I volunteered. The CO was desperate, and I was young and impatient to avoid the long work-up period. I just wanted to go, get some ribbons and stop wondering how I would react to be shot at.

Lt(jg) L E 'Rocky' Johnson of Det Lima in June 1966. Sporting various pockets and devices in his flight kit, Johnson was 'out for action' during these early cruises . . . and he certainly found it

A colourful leader of colourful men, Lt Cdr J M Schulze indulges in a little pre-flight whimsy wearing a Prussian spiked helmet. The Det Bravo OINC is well equipped with a shoulder holster, Mk-3C survival vest and large survival knife centrally mounted in the mid-chest position. Typical of the period, his torso harness uses a combination of upper koch fittings and older lap rocket-jet fittings

'Four weeks after I arrived aboard *Hancock*, the det lost another pilot, Lt John Helig (in RF-8G BuNo 146831) in May. He was shot down and taken prisoner. His replacement, Lt Cdr Len Eastman, was with us only two weeks before he, too, was shot down (in BuNo 146830) in June. He was also captured, and eventually returned.'

Like many photo pilots, Johnson realised how much responsibility VFP offered a junior aviator.

'I planned and led more than 100 flights into North Vietnam, where there were no rules except those of survival. I flew fast and low. What young kid doesn't dream about that?'

The basic survival caveats were: don't fly below 3000 ft, go very fast (more than 600 knots), and when you weren't actually taking pictures, keeping jinking.

Lt(jg) Johnson soon acquired a nickname after a particular mission on 26 May 1966. Scheduled for a road recce in the Thanh Hoa area, he found the weather marginal with low ceilings and showers. As he approached the city, his ECM gear started sounding its missile-launch warning. He went into a hard, descending turn and headed back over the water without seeing the SAM.

With weather obscuring his primary target, he chose his secondary, Nam Dinh. He crossed the coast at 500 ft, below the clouds. He could see a lot of activity as he flew over enemy territory. Typically, the North Vietnamese were taking advantage of the bad weather, which usually brought a respite from the intense air attacks, and were moving supply convoys of truck and trains south.

'I was excited to see the heavy truck and train activity', he said, 'and turned on my cameras'.

Busy flying so low and fast and operating his cameras, he didn't realise he was being overtaken by a swarm of tracers. Finally, he saw his danger and broke off his run. Still thinking he was much nearer the coast than he was, he headed due east. But after ten minutes, he still couldn't see the Gulf and now realised he was a lot further inland – and north. He took up a more south-easterly heading and after another ten minutes, he was 'feet wet'.

That evening, in the carrier's wardroom, one of his det's PI officers spread a large map out on the table where Lt(jg) Johnson and five other pilots were eating. The intelligence officer was obviously a little exasperated.

'Do you know where you were this afternoon?' he asked Johnson, who replied he thought he was near Thanh Hoa. Explaining it had taken his PI team several hours to piece things together, the PI said, no, Johnson had actually been over Hanoi! No wonder the fire was so heavy.

One of the other pilots shook his head and said, '"Rocky", the flying squirrel'. He was referring to the 'hero' of a popular television cartoon series – in truth, 'Rocky' was always level-headed, dedicated and patriotic, and it was his fumbling sidekick, 'Bullwinkle', the moose, who was usually confused! But Johnson received the Navy Commendation Medal with Combat 'V'.

'The citation said the intelligence was valuable, but it didn't mention I didn't know where I was, and that even if I had known, I shouldn't have been there.'

## *ORISKANY* FIRE

Besides the dangers of flying combat over heavily defended areas of North Vietnam, aviators also faced danger even when supposedly safe aboard their carrier. Fire is a constant threat for any ship's crew, and aircraft carriers have had their share of conflagrations. One of the most devastating was the fire that broke out in the early morning of 26 October 1966 on board *Oriskany*, which resulted in the deaths of 44 officers and men. The veteran ship was on the second of seven combat cruises during the Vietnam War.

Only nine months later, in July 1967, USS *Forrestal* (CVA-59) suffered a fire that killed 134, then in January 1969 a fire on board USS *Enterprise* (CVAN-65) took a further 27 lives.

The 1967 Det Bravo officers pose aboard *Hancock*. They are (front row), AZC R E Ward, Jr, Ens E F Miller, Ens J J Czekanski, Lt(jg) E H Haffey, and (rear row) Lt(jg) L E Johnson, Lt C M Clark, Lt Cdr J M Schulze and Lt R F Ball. AZC Ward was a chief petty officer (an enlisted NCO). The jet forming the backdrop for this photo (BuNo 146848) later became the third of eight RF-8Gs lost by VFP-63 between June 1976 and August 1977 when it crashed on 12 August 1976

The *Oriskany* and *Forrestal* tragedies resulted in a major overhaul of firefighting and survival training, including the use and maintenance of oxygen breathing apparatuses (OBAs).

One of those caught up in the *Oriskany* blaze was Lt Coltrin, who had faced enemy flak and SAMs strapped in an RF-8, but now found he had to deal with what was potentially the most fatal enemy of all aboard his own ship (the varied experiences of others that witnessed *Oriskany's* fire at first hand are told in the companion F-8 volume in this series);

'It was early morning. The pre-dawn launch had been scrubbed, and the "ordies" were downloading flares from the A-4s and preparing the aircraft for daylight operations. As two "red shirts" (ordnancemen) were taking the flares to the lockers, they decided to play catch. The fuse of one flare got pulled, and the flare ignited. Although the edge of the ship was not far away, in his panic, one of the airmen threw the burning flare into the flare locker instead of overboard. Before the sailor could shut the locker door and dog it down, the explosions started (it was never determined that the ignition of the flare started with a haphazard game. Rather, a mishandling of the Mk-24 flare resulted in its lanyard catching on something, followed by ignition – author).

'The first blast ripped the door open with such force that the dogs were torn out of the edge of the door like large bites. The door threw the sailor who was setting the dogs well clear before the first fireball emerged. The door then crushed a metal ladder behind it. Every few seconds, fireballs – with temperatures in the thousands of degrees – shot out the locker doorway like huge Roman candles and raced through the passageways of the ship. Oxygen and burnable material fed the fireballs as they went.

'I was asleep in my stateroom, one deck below the flight deck, when the fire alarm went off. When the alarm was called, my roommate and I

After the fire is safely out, crewmen cluster in groups on the wood-covered flight deck of the gutted *Oriskany* on 26 October 1966. A blackened A-4 is visible in the upper left of the photo. Some men gaze at a lowered deck-edge elevator, whilst in the foreground, legendary VF-162 skipper (and recent MiG killer), Cdr Dick Bellinger (shaven head, facing the camera), checks the status of his squadron with fellow officers

The scene on the smoking flight deck during the *Oriskany* fire showing clusters of A-4s and A-1s blackened by the blaze

thought it was another drill. We had been having a lot of those during the cruise, and I rolled over to go back to sleep. As a member of the air wing and not ship's company, I would let them play fire drill on their own. Shortly thereafter, my roommate got up saying, "I heard something that sounded like an explosion". He left the room.

'Still not too excited, I continued to try to sleep. Later, I heard the door open as someone came in. I heard a strange voice ask, "Is anyone here?" I asked who he was and he replied, "Seaman so-n-so" (I can't remember the name).

'I said, "Seaman, this is Lt Coltrin. What are you doing in my state-room?"

'He replied, "Sir, the ship is on fire and we are trapped!" I decided to get up! I went to the door and opened it. I could see nothing but thick smoke. I put my arms and hands out into the passageway, and they disappeared

Where it started – the flare locker shows the blowtorch effect of the inferno

in this white haze. I could feel many people lined up trying to get out of the area. It was too crowded to try to squeeze in. I went back into the room and shut the door.

'At the start of the cruise, my roommates and I had installed an air-conditioner in our room. We vented it into the head next door. It was very inefficient, so we had sealed every air leak we could find in the room to keep the cool air in. This now paid off by keeping the smoke out.

'I put on my Nomex flight pants and shirt (at this time, several squadrons had non-regulation gear obtained through swaps with Army units. *Oriskany*'s squadrons sported camouflaged flightsuits, as well as unofficial Nomex outfits and flight gear – author).

'The sailor went to the phone to call for help, and I went back to the door and checked the passageway. He said no help was available, and I found the passageway still jammed with people.

'The floor was starting to get hot and the tile was burning my feet, so I put on my flight boots. The smoke was now thick and heavy, and the room was very hot. We were being driven to the floor to breathe. I went to the sink and soaked two towels. I gave one to the sailor and I wrapped the other, a black one, around my head and said, "Let's go"

'As I opened the door, my companion darted to the left. I yelled to him that was a dead end, but he disappeared into the smoke. I went to the right. The passageway was now clear of people. The passageway led fore and aft. In about 15 ft it fed into a cross-ship passageway. I knew I was there when I ran into the knee-knocker. By this time, I knew the main fire was on the starboard side of the ship, so I turned right and headed to the port side. I did not turn fast enough and ran into a locker and smashed my hand. I later found out this locker contained OBAs, but it wouldn't have mattered because I didn't know how to use one. I wanted to continue down this passage until I reached the ladder that I knew went down to the hangar bay.

'At about the point that I should have been coming to the ladder, I became confused because the port-catapult room was now on fire. The flames from the catapult room mixed with the smoke and disoriented me. This problem turned out to be one of my luckier moments. A friend of mine, the air wing flight surgeon, found the ladder I was searching for. As he reached the first landing, the helicopter that was parked just below caught fire and roasted him on the spot.

'Unable to find the ladder, I continued to the end of the passageway knowing that there was a hatch there that led to a catwalk outside. I reached the hatch and found it dogged down. Scared, disoriented, and finding it very hard to breathe, I tried to undog the hatch. I thought I had undone all the dogs but the hatch would not open. I heard screams – I do not know whose, maybe mine. Frustrated and thinking I was going to die, I angrily kicked the hatch. To my great surprise, it opened. I stumbled out onto the catwalk and laid there a few seconds, breathing the air.

'I stood up and looked across the flight deck. There were only a few inches of clear air between the flight deck and the smoke layer. The skipper had turned the ship, putting the wind from the starboard side, blowing the smoke to port to increase the visibility on the starboard side to fight the larger fire more effectively.

'As I looked between the flight deck and the smoke, I saw the feet of two main groups of people. One group was near the island and the other near the fantail. I started crawling toward the group near the island. Suddenly to my right, I saw the CO of VF-111 crawling toward me.

'"Andre", he gasped, "do you have a cigarette? I'm dying for a smoke". I couldn't believe what I heard.

'I said, "Skipper, if you just raise your head three inches, you can get all the smoke you want".

'He said, "No, no, I need a cigarette", and crawled off. I continued crawling toward the island, where I checked in with the mustering officer and tried to see about the status of our detachment. Most everyone from the det had been accounted for. My roommate, who always wore a red-and-white striped night-gown to bed, looked very much out of place, but no one else seemed to notice.

'He had reached the cross-ship passageway but did not turn right or left. He continued straight ahead, and ended up in the admiral's quarters. He, the admiral and a member of the admiral's staff pulled off the air-vent cover. They gathered around this 4-to-6-inch opening, breathing what air they could. Since the admiral was the admiral, a rescue team soon arrived and led them all to safety.

'As I stood around, I noticed a lot of activity just forward of the island. Crews were pushing bombs and other explosives overboard. Men with OBAs were entering smoke-filled compartments to retrieve those explosives. They had wire-lead cables firmly attached to their backs in case they became incapacitated. People outside could then physically drag them to safety.

'I was very impressed by the bravery of these men. One of them was a young officer from VF-162, Lt(jg) Jim 'Flaps' (he had big ears) Andrews. He was willing to go anywhere and do anything. More than once while I was standing there, one of these brave men had to be dragged out of the compartment by his safety wire because he had been overcome by smoke. It was here that I learned how to put on, test, and use an OBA. Unfortunately, a very large percentage of them were not usable and were being thrown overboard.

'After my lesson, I joined a Marine and two "white hats" (enlisted sailors) on a search party. There were still a lot of people missing. I grabbed an untested OBA and followed them down a couple of decks. When I put on the OBA, I found it almost useless. Although it did produce oxygen, the eyepiece was so scratched I could barely see through it.

'We entered the dark, smoke-filled, passageways carrying a metal stretcher. It was very hot and muggy, and we were in water above our knees. It was worse than being in an oven.

'Every now and then, we would pass live electrical wires sparking off the water and bulkhead. As long as the wires were on our side and we did not go between two of them, we were supposedly safe. In water up to my knees, carrying a metal stretcher, with live electrical wires sparking around, and unable to see – I was not too confident.

'We found the stateroom of one of the missing officers. At first we thought no one was there but looking a more closely, we found a lump of something we realised had been a man. The heat had been so intense he had melted into an unidentifiable heap. His dentures could not even identify him (the process of elimination later identified him).

The photo in *Time*. During a mission on 9 February 1967, Lt(jg) Johnson caught Communist water traffic preparing to bring material south

'I helped carry a man out whom I did not think I knew. I thought he was black. He turned out to be a good friend that I had flown with many times. The fire had charred his skin and singed his hair. Only when we rolled him over and I saw his unburned side did I know who it was. This same pilot had survived two ejections earlier in the cruise.

'In one of the fighter ready rooms, the SDO received a call from some of his shipmates who were trapped in their stateroom on the third deck. He told them that all the rescue teams were very busy and that they would have to find their own way out. Shortly thereafter, there was a loud, horrible noise that sounded like uncontrollable screaming over the phone, then it suddenly went dead. We didn't know if it was the sound of the men being burned to death or a strange sound made by the phone lines as the wires melted. It made the hair on the back on every man's neck in that ready room stand on end. One man out of eight did escape from that room.

'As a couple of the men succumbed, an LDO (limited duty officer, a former enlisted man who had been commissioned in his area of speciality) from VF-111 decided he was not going die this way and busted out of the room. He raced to the ladder that took him to the second deck. As he was running blindly across the deck he passed out from the smoke. Falling to the floor, he regained consciousness, breathing the smoke-free air close to the deck.

'Getting to his feet, he again started running across the deck to the port side of the ship. Passing out again, he fell down a ladder to the third deck. At the bottom of the ladder, he accidentally slammed into the stateroom door of one of his shipmates, who had been able to sleep through all the previous commotion. The loud bang against his door woke him up.

'As he opened the door, he saw his friend and realised the dangerous situation. Throwing his unconscious shipmate over his shoulder, he carried him to the safety of the flight deck. They had saved each other's lives.

'Over on the port side of the ship, the helicopter crew was directing a fire crew on the flight deck on where to lower a fire hose to an open porthole a few decks down. In this stateroom was a pilot from one of the VA squadrons. As he had tried to exit his room he was met with huge balls of flames. He tried to escape a couple of times to no avail. He stuck his head out the porthole to breathe, and to put the fire hose that had been lowered to him over his shoulder, spraying down his back, while his stateroom burned around him. The only injury he received was a bruised knee caused by him banging it against the bulkhead trying to escape the heat.

Lt Ron Ball of Det Bravo was shot down on 19 April 1966 during a photo mission. After ejecting from his RF-8A (BuNo 146843), he was rescued by a SH-3A of HS-4 from USS *Yorktown*. He has inflated his personal flotation bags, and his survival radio dangles below the left bag

'A man was trapped in one compartment when the water used to fight the fire flooded it. The lights were out, and it was pitch black. As the water rose, the man shimmied up a pipe in the corner of the room to escape the rising water and to breathe. He stayed in this dark, torturous situation for hours before he was rescued. He suffered psychological trauma, but later recovered.

'Some time during my roaming around the ship, to my surprise I came across the sailor who had come to my stateroom. I had not expected to see him alive again. I asked him what happened after he left my stateroom and how he got out. He had tripped over the body of an officer who lived across the hall, which is why he disappeared so fast. He checked the downed officer to confirm he was dead, and then proceeded to the end of the passageway to a compartment where some of his friends worked. As it turned out they had already evacuated the area and he did likewise.

'During the fire, we received a lot of help and supplies from other carriers and ships that were on the line. And after what seemed like a very long time, the fire was under control and eventually put out completely. We headed for the Philippines. En route, we had a burial-at-sea ceremony. That was tough. It still raises goose bumps. The trip to the Philippines was very sombre. We couldn't escape the smell of death and burned flesh.'

Lt Coltrin made another cruise in *Oriskany* in 1967. After serving in several other squadron assignments, he got the chance to join VF-194, flying F-8Js, in 1970, with whom he made yet another deployment to the war zone. For personal reasons, he eventually resigned his regular Navy commission for one in the reserve, and soon became the OINC of a VFP-63 photo detachment aboard USS *Franklin D Roosevelt* (CVA-42).

This time, the cruise went to the relatively peaceful waters of the Mediterranean. However, the *FDR*, normally assigned to the Atlantic Fleet, had actually made a single combat cruise to Vietnam early on in the war, with a det from AIRLANT light-photo squadron VFP-62 as part of Air Wing 1.

Flying an RF-8G, VFP-62 aviator Lt Norman Green was on a mission on 6 September 1966, near the end of the *FDR*'s combat deployment. Making a final pass over shipping in Haiphong Harbour at more than 600 knots, Green felt his aircraft (BuNo 144615) shudder from a flak hit. He immediately thought that something had come off his RF-8G, and he was right – a 37 mm shell had shot off part of his outer left wing, and had also damaged the casing of the afterburner. His left aileron was gone as well. However, he was able to make a straight-in approach to the *Roosevelt* and recover safely. It was the only major damage to a photo-Crusader VFP-62 suffered in combat during the cruise.

VFP-63's Len Johnson enjoyed a brief moment of fame when a few of his mission photos appeared in the weekly news magazine, *Time*. On 9 February 1967, as a member of Det Bravo, he flew a reconnaissance mission during a cease-fire called by President Johnson as a goodwill gesture during the Tet lunar holiday. As Johnson commented, 'Although it might have been an easy day for the guys who dropped bombs, it was just another "day in the barrel" for the photo dets.'

Launching from *Hancock*, the young 'jaygee' headed for Vinh. Fog covered the entire Vietnam coast, and it was hard to see how far inland the blanket extended. The fog reached as high as 5000 ft, and as on so many other missions, Johnson nevertheless decided to try to find the base. He levelled out at what his radar altimeter said was 50 ft. He could see the waves right under his speeding aircraft. Not a good place to be.

He climbed and reversed his course, heading back out to sea. Fiddling with his radio for possible information on targets of opportunity, Johnson heard a report of major ground activity on an Air Force frequency. Receiving a position report, Johnson took his escort down toward this new target, which turned out to be major movement of troops, trucks and boats on a river.

There were large amounts of supplies on either bank and lots of trucks. Ferry boats dotted the water as the American reconnaissance jet flashed above the surprised North Vietnamese, barely 1500 ft over their heads. The Communists opened up with everything they had. Johnson made two runs over the area, then turned for home.

Back at the ship, the enthusiastic intel officers and men poured over the new film.

'I was interested', Johnson recalls, 'and spent more time than usual looking at the film. I usually gave my pictures a quick look, but this time I was fascinated to see the enemy in such detail.'

The interpreters wrote their reports and sent them, along with the film, to Hawaii and the Pacific fleet air intelligence centre. Johnson forgot about the mission. But two weeks later, while he thumbed through a new issue of *Time*, he saw an article about the Tet stand-down, and how the enemy was using it to re-supply their people in South Vietnam.

'The accompanying photos for the article looked familiar. Hey! They were mine!'

The photograph also appeared in *US News & World Report*, as well as *Life*. Johnson subsequently received the Distinguished Flying Cross for that mission.

**PP 931 launches from *Bonnie Dick* in 1965**

**Fifteen years after his first combat missions, now-Cdr L E Johnson prepares to fly a mission in an RF-8G of VFP-306, which he commanded in 1981. Items of interest include the pantagraph reticule for air-to-air photography (just above Johnson on the canopy) and the stall-warning stick-shaker below his right hand on the aircraft's fuselage**

# GETTING THE COVERAGE

Unfortunately, with all the heroic and dedicated efforts of the men and ships of TF 77, including the almost non-stop missions of the RF-8s, the Communists were in no mood to talk, and the war continued. By late 1967, the North Vietnamese embarked on a large operation that sent huge amounts of supplies south for a big military offensive in early 1968. With a holiday stand-down and peace bargaining schemes emanating from Washington, most of the intense strikes ceased. But the RF-8 dets flew on and on, and on.

VFP-63's Lt Lou Mortimer had established a routine in his first deployment;

'Because of the holidays, we thought everyone would enjoy a stand-down. But, not us in photo. I never worked so hard in my life. We flew mission after mission. Before, I would look at film and never see anything. But during the Christmas Truce, it was open season. The roads were full of trucks, even during the day, all moving south. We reported all that, projecting where it would be at nightfall.

'While the air wing flew mainly around the ship, like on CAP missions, our RF-8s were flying regular missions. I looked at stacks of film, wrote my reports, only to look up and find more stacks waiting for me. One day,

The 1967 VFP-63 *Coral Sea* det after the loss of the original OINC, Lt Cdr James Vescelius. They are (rear row, left to right), Lt(jg) Jay Miller, Lt(jg) Gordie Paige, Lt(jg) Lou Mortimer and Lt(jg) Will Gray. Front row (left to right), Lt(jg) Phil Sherman, Lt Curt Eininger and Lt Cdr Bill Rosson. Miller attained flag rank, while Paige (by now a lieutnant-commander) became the last F-8 PoW in 1972, requiring now-Lt Cdr Gray to replace him as OINC in the photo det aboard *Midway*. Mortimer and Eininger were the det intelligence officers

67

The infamous Thanh Hoa Bridge during a CVW-16 strike in 1967. In reality a somewhat rickety old railway crossing, this bridge became a symbol of the frustration felt by many Navy and Air Force pilots. It also highlighted the North Vietnamese resiliency and ability to repair damage to major facilities seemingly overnight

I worked 24 hours around the clock to get the film processed and out during that period.

'Of course, all this stuff went to supply the 1968 Tet Offensive, an all-out Communist drive against the south. During Tet, the ship went south from *Yankee Station* to support defences against the Tet drive, on *Dixie Station.*'

The big Communist offensive finally began on 30 January 1968, throughout South Vietnam, and the intensity of the attacks still evokes strong emotions 20 years later. This period of heavy fighting included the legendary defence of a small US Marine outpost at Khe Sanh, six miles from the Laotian border. Much of the supplies for the Communist drive came down the trails from the north, watched and reported by the faithful RF-8 photo dets.

However, the Communist offensive failed, and the air strikes continued as before. The American government was determined to bring the North Vietnamese to the peace table, and offered several so-called 'bombing halts' as inducements. The most far-reaching of these pauses was the halt begun on 1 November. President Lyndon Johnson decreed there would be no further strikes into North Vietnam. It was a desperate gamble by a president who had decided not to seek re-election, but that gamble also failed.

Lt(jg) (later Rear Admiral) Jay Miller saw service as a VFP-63 photo-

Crusader pilot in two TF 77 carriers during two eventful combat tours;

'The "Alpha's" trimetrogen camera was actually three separate cameras in Station 2. There was another set of windows that subsequently disappeared, two that looked obliquely and one, vertically. If you ran with 3-inch lenses, you got almost a panoramic view. The three cameras took separate pictures with good overlap. The photo-intelligence specialists made prints, then a mosaic. The other cameras were 70 mm, with 3-, 6-, and 12-inch lenses. So, the 12-inch lens and 70 mm frame was the same as a 24-inch lens on a 4-inch frame – telephoto city! The film resolution wasn't very good, though.

'By the time I flew the RF-8A in VFP-63, it was being replaced in the fleet by the RF-8G. I liked the A better, however. It didn't have the G's ventral strakes, and I could put it in a skid. It was easy to hold it in a skid to follow a railroad track that moved away from you. If you put in full rudder and full rudder trim, that sucker would skew around sideways. It would nearly fly through the air *sideways*.

'Vought put the strakes on the plane for stability but we didn't need stability for our mission. Without ventral fins, we flew better missions.'

Richard Coffman, a career VFP pilot who also spent a tour as a test pilot at Patuxent, agreed that the RF-8A's skidding ability was an asset during a mission. However, the RF-8G's larger engine and increased speed, which could approach 700 knots flat out, required the stability provided by the strakes, even though the G's jinking ability was reduced.

Jay Miller continues;

'Half-way through my tour with -63, we got automatic exposure control, which was no good. If you flew over a broken cloud deck, the cameras exposed against the available light on the top of the clouds. If your target appeared through a three-mile-wide hole in the clouds, all the available light would close down your camera's aperture, and the picture of the ground would be underexposed. With manual exposure, I could raise the aperture a half-stop to compensate and return with beautiful pictures. As is often the case, automation has its drawbacks.

'The Crusader's cameras were very reliable. I don't think I had five failures during my combat tours. And the photomates were phenomenal. They rebuilt the cameras right on the ship. We had a repairman besides the PHs, and we just didn't have camera or film failures. No processor failures, either. It was a slick operation. VFP-63 had one hell of a reputation for bringing back the product. It was a thoroughly enjoyable mission.'

Miller had originally wanted to be an A-6 pilot. He had top flight grades, but at the time, only second-tour returning aviators got Intruder seats. However, one of his instructors had been a photo pilot, and he suggested Miller consider that community. It was an exacting, exciting, mission, the instructor said, fun to fly, and a little out of the ordinary. This appealed to Ens Miller, and he requested RF-8 training, much to the surprise of his assignment detailers.

'They probably dropped their teeth when they saw my request for photos', he laughed. Later on, however, it became clear that the career path for recon pilots was not a smooth one. When his obligatory service ended, Miller left active duty to become an airline pilot. He also joined the Naval Air Reserve, where he continued his association with the

RF-8G, and eventually became the commanding officer of VFP-206 – the last US Crusader squadron. After several subsequent assignments, he was selected for flag rank.

### 'CORKTIPS' IN COMBAT

Navy squadrons have at least two nicknames, one popular, and the other tactical. VFP-63 was widely known as 'The Eyes of the Fleet', alluding to its photo-reconnaissance mission. However, a second squadron name – its radio callsign – was 'Corktip', which had nothing to do with the mission or individual pilots. The tactical callsign was used strictly for mission-related transmissions, and was chosen so that it would not conflict with another squadron's sign. Thus, when a VFP-63 pilot called 'Corktip 710, feet wet', listeners knew a VFP driver was over the water, probably returning from his mission.

Jay Miller's first combat tour was with Det 43 in CVW-15, aboard the *Coral Sea*. The veteran carrier sailed from San Francisco in late July 1967, and after work-ups in Hawaii, began combat operations off Vietnam. It was an eventful cruise, involving many of the heaviest strikes of the war. Several flight crews were lost, killed, or posted missing in action, many of them becoming prisoners of war. A few days after the first combat strikes, Jay Miller's det lost its officer-in-charge (OINC).

Lt Cdr Jim Vescelius was covering a strike when he was shot down. He apparently ejected and landed on the ground, where he was surrounded by North Vietnamese. Although the story cannot be verified, it is believed that Vescelius tried to draw his service pistol, perhaps to fight it out with the advancing enemy troops, who shot him dead on the spot. At any rate, he did not return with the prisoners in 1973.

Jay Miller received the Distinguished Flying Cross for a mission on 28 September 1967 – a week after Vescelius was lost – during a heavy strike against the main port city of Haiphong. The intense flak did not deter the

After the Easter Invasion of March 1972, many previously restricted targets were hit in an all-out campaign against the road and railways systems that carried supplies south. Although the 1966-68 *Rolling Thunder* strikes had damaged many of these supply arteries, the 1972 strikes saw greatly intensified attacks, including this one in April 1972 by aircraft from the *Hancock* against the Dong Phong Thuong Bridge

NL 710 (BuNo 144618) gets the launch signal during the *Coral Sea* combat cruise in 1967. This photo, taken in October, shows the pilot's braced position immediately before the cat stroke. The Crusader is also in tension, cocked slightly nose up on the catapult, with the bridles attached to the shuttle immediately behind the nosegear. The name below the canopy is that of Lt(jg) Will Gray. This aircraft survived a further 15 years of fleet service (including a round-the-world deployment with *Independence* as part of VFP-63 Det 4 in 1980-81) before finally being retired to Davis-Monthan on 15 April 1982

young pilot from getting the necessary post-strike photography, and the wing commander, Cdr James Linder, recommended Miller for the DFC. Linder, himself, received the Navy Cross, second only to the Medal of Honor, for leading the strike.

Here, Miller describes a sortie over the infamous Thanh Hoa Bridge;

'The first time over the bridge, I saw the twinkle of the flak guns. They had perhaps six to eight mounts by a big rock formation. Our flight path flew right over those sites. The bridge was not a tactical target. It was totally useless at that time, in early 1968. CVW-15 had gotten a reputation as "the bridge busters", and Cdr Linder wanted to further that mystique. He got permission for a wing strike on Thanh Hoa. Actually, I doubt you could have walked safely across the bridge. It was just framework. A rail maybe every 20 yards, but the iron framework had received a lot of attention from the Navy and Air Force. Cdr Linder wanted to knock it down so there would be a hole in the river.

'The North Vietnamese also believed a legend that the bridge held their country together. As long as it remained intact, they would be strong. One raid dropped underwater concussion bombs. Half of them went all over the countryside. The bridge didn't look any different. I probably went over that bridge 50 times, because whenever you were in that part of the world, you took photos of Thanh Hoa.

'The Vietnamese had 37 mm and 57 mm gun sites at the bridge because there was always some jerk pilot willing to go after it when he had a bomb left. They *did* have transhipment points (ferry points) up and down the river. So, they did use that part of the river, although not the bridge, itself.

'The first trip by, we saw the guns sparkling, the muzzle flashes – 37 mm, 57 mm, pom-pom. Nothing bigger, and no SAMs. Earlier in the war, when the bridge was still serviceable, it was heavily defended. That's where it got its reputation.

'We followed the strike group in, about three miles from the water. The bombers went in with a few flak suppressors. While they coasted in toward the bridge, I was maybe 20 miles south. In that area, Vietnam was about five minutes wide, the way we flew. Then you were in Laos. I hooked a big U-turn, and I could see and hear the bombers pulling off. When they were "feet wet", I told my escort to come up the river at 500-550 knots, toward the water. I picked up the river, probably 7-8 miles before the bridge. I didn't want to end up with less than a perfect picture because of all the interest CAG Linder had generated. I told myself I was just going to fly right over that damn thing, wings level, because I wasn't going to worry about any really big reaction from the people on the ground.

'I was set up *hours* ahead. I was still back on the ship planning the mission. It was so simple compared to other stuff. Maybe that was my problem. Bouncing along at 550 knots, you're having a big time. Here comes the bridge, and they start firing.

'I went over the bridge – saw it go through the viewfinder – and that's when I looked down at the counters, after I hit the water. I'd loused up. I was probably between 3500 and 6000 ft – 3500 out of small arms range, and 6000 max because of my cameras. The pictures were tough to read above 6000. So, I was probably at 4500 ft minimum.

'I probably wasn't in afterburner, either. The RF-8G would hit 550 in basic engine if you weren't pulling on it – no Gs, that sort of stuff. We seldom used 'burner over the beach because we'd go supersonic so quickly. Then we'd get a nose tuck. If you were not in the cockpit flying the altitude, the nose would tuck *up*, and you could change 1000 ft altitude if you weren't watching your altimeter.

'If your computer was set up the road for 5000 ft and 550 knots, the grid in the viewfinder was tracking nicely, and you rammed the throttle into 'burner – you did a 500-ft "whifferdill". The only time I used 'burner was if someone was shooting at me, or if we were going over Haiphong. Then, I'd set up for 'burner well in advance so that I didn't have to make any transitions close to the target. I'd been supersonic over downtown Haiphong, which made sense. I always assumed the greater the speed, the greater the problem for the guys on the ground shooting at me. Most of their aiming was optical.'

While perhaps grimly humorous, one of Miller's missions illustrates what could happen if the predictability of recon flights was altered. He launched from *Coral Sea* with an F-4B escort to take post-strike photography of a another mission against the Thanh Hoa Bridge in 1968. The bomber force hit the bridge amidst a barrage of anti-aircraft fire. Within a predictable minute or two of the strike force's departure, the photo pilot made his run over the target, meeting the same heavy fire, this time concentrating on one aircraft.

Finishing his run, the Crusader pilot rejoined the Phantom II, which had stood off to intercept possible MiG threats to the RF-8, as well as to provide instant air cover should the recon jet be shot down.

Lt(jg) Miller cleared his throat and informed his escort pilot, Lt Cdr Pete Purvis, that he had 'a problem or two', and that it was necessary to refly the run.

Actually, Miller had forgotten to turn on his camera switches, and had not gotten any coverage of the target. Since the strike was of special interest to the carrier group commander, coverage was mandatory – however, there were fuel considerations, as well as the thought of flying back through the flak area. Nevertheless, the RF-8 driver turned around and hastily flew over the bridge once more, getting the necessary photography. Amazingly, no flak rose toward him. The reason was obvious – the people on the ground were not expecting the photo-bird to make a second run, and so had relaxed their vigilance.

Obviously, if other reconnaissance pilots had been allowed to vary their individual times over the target, especially after a large strike, many men would have been recovered safely aboard their carriers instead of being lost, or becoming prisoners of war.

Following his 1967-68 combat tour with CVW-15, Miller returned to NAS Miramar at San Diego, in California. He volunteered for another Vietnam tour and flew out to the *Bon Homme Richard* already midway through a cruise. Actually, he and another pilot 'transpaced' two RF-8s from San Diego across the Pacific, through Hawaii, Wake, Guam and the Philippines – no mean feat of navigation and simple pilot fortitude. He joined CVW-5 and quickly got back into combat.

On 1 August 1968 Miller and his escort, Lt Norm McCoy of VF-51, were returning from a mission. They had just gone 'feet wet' when they got a call that another F-8 needed a replacement for his wingman who had had to return to the ship. Since he was over the water, and safe from any MiG threat, Miller released his escort to join on the solo fighter. As Miller and the rest of the wing listened, however, the normally routine CAP quickly became anything *but* routine.

As soon as McCoy joined on squadronmate Lt George Hise, they got a vector toward an in-coming MiG-21. Although Hise may have damaged the MiG, it was Norm McCoy's Sidewinder that apparently sent the North Vietnamese fighter down – at least that was the way the wing commander ruled after listening to the tape that Jay Miller had recorded during the engagement.

On 31 October 1968, frustrated and out of ideas, President Johnson, who that March had declared he would not seek another term, called a unilateral bombing halt against all targets in the north. It was the last major wartime decision of this angry, internationally inept, president. The halt had far-reaching implications for all the servicemen who remained in South-East Asia. Just at the point when, to them at least, it appeared that their daily raids were having some effect on the Communists, their 'fangs had been pulled' and their 'weapons sheathed'. The enemy had received a reprieve that would let them re-arm and resuscitate themselves in relative peace. The North Vietnamese knew it, and so did the frustrated, angry men in the cockpits up and down the South China Sea.

Yet, as in other such bombing halts, while the other squadrons in the carrier air wings reoriented their attentions to the south, or withdrew from combat entirely, the light-photo dets continued flying missions to monitor Communist compliance with the truce. There were reprisal raids, authorised only after the RF-8s and RA-5s had been shot at.

Even with the far-reaching bombing halt, the photo-birds were in danger. On 3 December 1968, Lt(jg) Jim Ozbirn, from the latest VFP-63

As a 'jaygee' in 1968, James Ozbirn had duelled with a SAM. Here, ten years later, now-Cdr Ozbirn strides toward his RF-8G at NAF Washington. Note his all-black flight helmet and barely distinguishable yellow flash, related to his callsign of 'Wizard'

73

Det 43, duelled with a North Vietnamese SAM as he approached the Ca River.

'I saw a missile rising out of low-lying fog near Vinh', he reported. 'It was far enough away so that I had plenty of time to take evasive action and avoid it. The missile exploded in a large ball of fire a couple of hundred feet away from my aircraft. I was two miles away from the coast, and I turned back inland and finished my photo run.'

VF-111's Dick Schaffert again;

'One of the classics to emerge from those days was a recording of the radio transmissions, *and heavy breathing*, of a photo "beanie" evading a SAM . . .'

A major development in the RF-8 community was the decommissioning of VFP-62 on 5 January 1968. After more than 100 detachments in 22 carriers during 19 years of service, VFP-62 retired. This change affected the entire reconnaissance community as other squadrons were decommissioned, including VAP-62 on 15 October 1969, and its sister squadron VAP-61 on 1 July 1971. These squadrons had given yeoman service in Vietnam with their RA-3Bs.

With the demise of VFP-62, VFP-63 now assumed responsibility for providing RF-8 dets to all the Navy's carriers world-wide, but the emphasis remained in Vietnam. In 1971, the squadron was restructured to include a permanent shore command – the 'home guard' – and five numbered detachments, with two dets for Atlantic operations, and three for the Pacific Fleet.

In addition, on 1 September 1972 VFP-63 assumed responsibility for all F-8 training in the Navy. VF-124, long known as 'Crusader College', began to gear up for the F-14 Tomcat, which was then in the early stages of flight testing. VFP-63 had received F-8Hs in 1969, with the idea being for the unit to provide its RF-8s with their own 'in-house' escorts. However, the requirements in the fleet necessitated redistributing the 'Hotels'

A line-up of Crusader tails from the *Oriskany* in August 1971 at NAS Atsugi, Japan. Two RF-8Gs (the aircraft at the extreme right of the photo is just visible) of VFP-63 flank fighters of VF-194, with the latter squadron's 'Red Diamonds' on their rudders. BuNo 146892 later became the second of eight VFP-63 jets lost in 1976-77, crashing on 15 July 1976, whilst BuNo 145636 (last in line-up) was lost in a crash exactly a year after this photo was taken when, on 1 August 1972, it crashed in the USA during a training flight (*Hideki Nagakubo*)

to fighter squadrons, and VFP-63 had to wait until the mid-1970s to get fighters once more. By that time, however, the F-8 had left the fleet, and the fighters saw employment as squadron hacks and currency trainers instead.

Lt(jg) (later Captain) Will Gray was a member of the *Coral Sea*'s 1967 photo det along with Jay Miller;

'Generally, the big threat to the photo pilot was AAA sector-barrage fire over the target. SAMs were rarely fired at us, and as far as I know only one RF-8 was ever attacked by MiGs. The escort shot the MiG, and the photo-bird returned safely to the ship (on 9 July 1968, VF-191's Lt Cdr John Nichols got a MiG-17 that appeared to be starting an attack run on the RF-8G he was protecting).

'I remember one particular mission where the AAA was really thick over Haiphong. It was a hazy day with a high overcast so the tracers looked like red rain. I got my pictures and decided it was time to turn right (I always turned right because most guys turned left).

'I was doing about 1.2 Mach as I had come downhill from 35,000 ft in 'burner for the run that was only about two minutes long. I was as scared as I have ever been in my life, and really laid in a good turn. Suddenly, I couldn't see very good. My eyes scanned the G meter – I had tunnel vision really bad – and the needle was sitting on the stop, more than 10 Gs. I lost 200 knots in that 100° turn while in 'burner.

'With a 6.4-G limit and only 5.1-G rolling, I had really put a hard lick on that bird. Thank goodness Vought built it so tough. I don't know why it didn't come apart and kill me. We found the port outer wing panel was basically destroyed with all the ribs inside broken into little pieces. I still believe that if I hadn't made that turn, I would have been shot down.

'Most of my 117 missions over North Vietnam I always ran above 600 knots and went into 'burner as needed to keep the speed up. I set the cam-

Squadrons usually maintained small shore detachments in Japan so that aircraft could be flown to these facilities for major maintenance and repair. Here, RF-8G BuNo 145636 from *Oriskany*'s 1971 cruise rests at NAS Atsugi. Note the tie-down chains on the Crusader's landing gear (*Hideki Nagakubo*)

era controls on the computer prior to ingress at 650 knots and 4000 ft, and turned the travelling grid in the viewfinder off so I could see the ground clearly. I did most of my work with the KA-53 12-inch lens camera and a KA-68 3-inch pan. Jinking was natural as just keeping the roads and rivers in the viewfinder caused you to really move around. On straight roads, I would vary the altitude. They would always shoot at you, but Vinh, Vin Son, Thanh Hoa and the larger towns were the really hot spots.

'I was mighty careful in my planning and execution – as careful as an ignorant young ensign can be. It seemed to me that most of the guys who were shot down violated some good rule about combat. Never go to the same place twice on the same sortie, never go below 3500 ft, always go as fast as your mission fuel would allow, don't fly through, or near, clouds, and never get caught over an overcast.

'Also, no matter what you thought about the sortie, "they were always shooting" was a good philosophy – and jink for one gun just as you would for 1000. Anyone who didn't respect those guys on the ground was stupid and in great peril.'

Gray's notes on personal equipment are of interest;

'I carried no personal items of any kind, other than my Browning 9 mm pistol. No rings or photos. We all used our "combat wallets" made by the riggers – a simple folded pouch to carry our ID, Geneva convention card, and some money. We did not wear patches on our flight gear, and only

**Although aerial refuelling by carrier aircraft is usually accomplished by designated carrier-borne tankers, shore-based tankers occasionally do the job also. Here, a Marine Corps KC-130 refuels VFP-63 Crusader BuNo 144613 from VFP-63 Det 1 over the Gulf of Tonkin in 1971. This aircraft later became the penultimate RF-8 lost to enemy action in Vietnam when it was shot down by AAA on 16 June 1972 whilst on a sortie from Midway as part of the carrier's Det 3. Its pilot, Lt P Ringwood, was recovered. However, when the det OINC, Lt Cdr G C Paige, was shot down in BuNo 146873 36 days later, they could not prevent him from becoming a PoW**

Seen in March 1971, an F-8J of VF-24 escorts a near-identically marked RF-8G of VFP-63 Det 1 during a photo mission over Vietnam from their TF 77 carrier, USS *Hancock*. Some 13 years later, BuNo 146845 became one of the last RF-8Gs retired to Davis-Monthan by VFP-306, the jet arriving in Arizona (as ND 604) on 25 September 1984 – just five days prior to the reserve unit's decommissioning at NAF Washington D.C.

our ship's laundry mark on our clothing. Our dog tags were tied into our shoe laces, too.'

While a number of Vietnam-era Crusader pilots flew from the larger *Midway*-class ships, the bulk of them counted their hours aboard the small 27C *Essexes*. Will Gray was one of the latter, completing a short cruise in *Shangri-la* (CVS-38);

'That was my only 27C experience in the Crusader, which was too much aeroplane for such a small deck. One guy blew lots of tyres, and finally a strut. Another strung out 25 OKs (a good landing grade), hit the ramp on his next trap, then recovered out with 17 more OKs. APC (approach power compensator) kept us alive on those little ships. People who chose to fly manual blew tyres and hit things.'

## NIXON IN THE WHITE HOUSE

President Richard M Nixon returned the Republicans to the White House in January 1969. His election came after years of intense US involvement in Vietnam. There were American ground troops in South Vietnam, plus massive US naval and air forces supporting them in Thailand, the Philippines and Guam, with the mighty US Seventh Fleet offshore. Despite these seemingly overwhelming forces in-theatre, perhaps the strongest shaping factor in the new administration's future foreign policy was the noisy, and sometimes violent, domestic public outcry.

Massive demonstrations in Washington, D.C., and several large

American cities had inhibited the Johnson Administration from taking any decisive step toward a military solution to the war. With the North Vietnamese seemingly unafraid of the massive American power arrayed against them, and the resulting stalemate, the incoming Nixon Administration was faced with very few alternatives, so it chose large-scale withdrawal.

Throughout the first half of 1969, air operations concentrated in South Vietnam in observance of the bombing halt imposed the preceding November, centring mainly in the so-called 'I Corps' area immediately south of the DMZ.

To safely conduct reconnaissance missions, armed escorts, A-4 'Iron Hand' anti-SAM aircraft, an A-4 RESCAP, available Marine radar jammers and Navy tankers were all tasked with protecting the photo-bird. The need for reconnaissance aircraft was so great during this period that the production line for the RA-5C Vigilante was reopened for the manufacture of 46 additional aircraft, bringing the total number of Vigilantes produced to 140.

Twenty-three RF-8As were also included in the programme, including the RF-8A of Maj John H Glenn – BuNo 144608 – which the famous Marine astronaut (and Senator) flew in his 1957 transcontinental flight. Glenn's Crusader was modified to RF-8G standards and issued to VFP-63, but was eventually lost off the *Oriskany* in 1973.

The war continued in the south, with occasional incursions into the north. President Nixon announced on 8 May 1970, during a meeting with South Vietnamese President Thieu, that he was ordering a phased withdrawal of American troops – 25,000 men had been recalled from South Vietnam by 29 August. Over the next year, more than 100,000 troops were pulled out of South Vietnam. But, the Navy's carriers remained on station.

# 1972-75 – THE LAST CAMPAIGNS

By the end of 1971, the war was beginning to heat up – not that the fighting on the ground had stopped with Johnson's 1968 bombing halt. Various short campaigns, especially into surrounding areas in Laos and Cambodia, had kept the conflict going. Only the intensity of American air raids had slackened. But renewed Communist activity had brought on increased bombing missions. US reconnaissance efforts kept a watch on the busy jungle trails as men and supplies kept flowing south. With the advent of the New Year, it was plain the North Vietnamese were ready to go for broke.

The 'flood' started on Easter Weekend, 25 March 1972, and in short order the North Vietnamese regular army and the Viet Cong rebel insurgents were punching through various important South Vietnamese positions. It was clear the South could not hold out without renewed American support. Air Force and Marine Corps units from Japan and the

The veteran 27C carrier USS *Ticonderoga* during a 1969 war cruise. New A-7B Corsair IIs VA-25 and VA-87 share the flight deck with F-8s of VF-111 and VF-162, RF-8s of VFP-63 and A-4s, which the A-7 was then replacing as the Navy's main light-attack bomber

US were recalled, and more Navy aircraft carriers were pulled back into the South China Sea.

As before, the 'big deck' carriers – *Enterprise*, *Constellation*, *Ranger*, *America* (CVA-66) and *Saratoga* (CVA-60), on temporary duty from the Atlantic Fleet – included RVAH squadrons of RA-5C Vigilantes as their reconnaissance aircraft. Although several 27C carriers had retired, *Hancock* and *Oriskany* were still in service. While they had begun changing some of their veteran A-4s for A-7s, they still carried two F-8 fighter squadrons, and an RF-8 det. *Coral Sea* and *Midway* also carried RF-8G photo dets.

Now-Lt Cdr Will Gray returned to the war as OINC for VFP-63's Det 3 to replace his roommate on his first two cruises, Lt Cdr Gordie Paige. Paige had been shot down on 22 July in RF-8G BuNo 146873, this aircraft becoming the last Crusader to be lost in combat;

'The war was just the same as it had been in 1967. If I had saved my maps I could have used them all over again. I always used charts, even though I knew the country like my own farm in Louisiana. I had a full set of charts, in every scale (1:5,000,000, 1:1,000,000, 1:250,000 and 1:50,000) for the target areas. There was no storage place for all that in the Crusader's cockpit, so I sat on the pile and kept the one I needed up in the windscreen.

'The only difference between my 1967 cruise in the *Coral Sea* and the 1972 cruise in the *Midway* was time, and a few minor equipment changes. I still flew the RF-8G, with different cameras and newer ECM gear. The escorts were still F-4s, with the same fuel problems. The F-4 was a hindrance because it was short on fuel, and because of its large radar cross-section and smoking exhaust, it alerted the enemy defences.

'When we had photo-on-photo escorts, we drew little fire. We jinked and flew fast. Our small radar cross-section did not present an offensive threat to the enemy, so he could not always come after us with his best shot.

'There were three carriers in the Gulf of Tonkin that had RF-8 dets, so I had to use a new callsign for my det. Instead of the familiar "Corktip",

The officers and CPO of *Tico*'s Det 14 in front of one of the home guard's aircraft in January 1969 back at Miramar. They are, from left to right, AEC W G Brag, Lt(jg) J S Nixdorff, Lt R L Coffman, Lt Cdr F A Grant, Lt D M Sjnuggerud, Lt(jg) L R Mortimer and Lt(jg) L F Boline. Nixdorff and Mortimer were the two det PIOs and Lt Cdr Grant the det OINC

we were now "Baby Giant". And our familiar Papa Papa (PP) tailcode letters were replaced with November Foxtrot (NF).

'The North Vietnamese defences were virtually the same except for one encounter I had with a ZSU-23. I was running a section of railroad that crossed the Thanh Hoa Bridge. I approached the bridge from the north at about 600 knots and 4500 ft. I was looking through the viewfinder, following the rail line, when I looked up to see a solid red line coming right at me from a point on the ground right by the railroad. I just about broke my right leg getting in rudder to break away. They missed! It was over in a second, but I was impressed. It took me a couple of miles to get back on the route and continue south until my Phantom II escort ran low on fuel and called, "Bingo!"

'One of the nicest features of the RF-8G was its great fuel load. With 10,152 lbs of JP-5 and a very low drag airframe, it had the perfect combination for photo work. The maximum trap fuel was low in those days because of older landing gear. You could only bring back about 2000 lbs of fuel.

'We always started late in the launch to save fuel, and took virtually no time to call, "Up and ready". We had no INS (Inertial Navigation System) to align and no crew to co-ordinate. Since the RF-8 was lighter than the fighter F-8, we generally made military power cat shots, which saved even more fuel.

'Saving fuel has to be a philosophy. We met our escorts on the KA-3 – the greatest tanker ever built – and waited for the F-4 to take on about 2000 lbs to top off. We flew to the coast-in point at about 31,000 ft at max-endurance speed to save fuel and eat up the clock. When we found the coast-in point, we pushed up the power and dumped the noses to gain speed before entering any SAM envelopes.

81

'I raised the droops passing about 400 KIAS, and the Crusader would run right up to Mach 1 at military power. The F-4 would generally have to go in and out of 'burner and play the inside of our turns to keep in position.'

On 10 November 1972 Gray launched in RF-8G BuNo 146876 for a road recce near Thanh Hoa. Another photo-Crusader had also launched for a separate mission, and after completing his run, Gray heard that the second RF-8 was having mechanical trouble, so he called the ship to tell them that he would fly this mission as well, having briefed with the other pilot.

The target was a MiG-17 field near Vinh, and as he and his F-4 escort approached, Gray began jinking to throw off any flak gunners who might be tracking him. Sure enough, his radar homing and warning (RHAW) gear soon indicated that he was indeed being 'painted', but there was no other threat. He began setting up for his run.

By now he was in a slight dive, going Mach 1. He wanted to get pictures of the runway with his KA-51 and KA-53 cameras, which shot straight down beneath the aircraft from stations 3 and 4 in the belly of the Crusader. Even though he was shooting out bundles of chaff, Gray knew the enemy radar still had him locked up. Soon, streams of tracers were heading toward him. He could even tell that the gun barrels were pointing ahead of him, leading him;

'Even though the cameras were running at nearly six frames a second, it all seemed to slow down. Fear like that makes time expand. I knew those boys on the ground were shooting only at me. I could see the bullets and the puffs of the exploding shells in my rear-view mirrors. Yes, I could hear them, too, even above Mach 1.'

Gray reached the end of the runway and made a hard turn south, then east toward the coast, and safety. He left the flak guns behind, but in a few minutes, another radar signal came up, this time from a SAM site. Chaff did not have much effect on these powerful radars, and he knew his only defence was to climb and keep his speed up.

With the F-4 crew hanging with him, the photo pilot streaked for the Gulf of Tonkin, hoping the North Vietnamese would not launch a missile. But his RHAW again lit up, indicating a SAM launch;

'I could see the booster flame and a big cloud of dust rising in the air. I began a climbing turn toward the missile to see if it was coming my way. I lost sight of it for a few seconds when the booster dropped off, but I soon saw the missile headed for me.'

A second missile also came up from the launch site, which was about 15 miles away. Gray headed for the first SAM at the speed of sound. The SA-2 was going Mach 4, giving more than 3000 knots of closure.

Manoeuvring as hard as he could, he finally overcame the missile, but not before the huge rocket blew past so close he could see the small forward fins and other details on the 35 ft-long smoking cylinder. The shock waves from the missiles rocked the two Navy jets as the SAMs blew up.

After returning to the carrier, Gray looked at his film with the PIs;

'The photos were good except for the last frame of the runway. It was blurred because of my hard roll to the left.'

Will Gray summed up his feelings about the Crusader, particularly the photo-bird;

'If you had to go to war, the Crusader was right for the job. Fast, manoeuvrable, easy on the fuel, and a bit stealthy – its heart was the J-57 engine, reliable and forgiving. The Crusader was hard to land aboard ship and very difficult to max perform in air combat, but for flat-out running in the world of the photo pilot, it was a real sweetheart. With the droops up in a descent, followed by a good shove from the hard-lighting afterburner, the airspeed spun up toward 700 knots indicated like a video game, only this was real.

'Only the high-speed fighter pilot knows what it feels like to be running at high speed. You can feel the power . . .'

## THE LAST MISSIONS

With the cease-fire of 27 January 1973, American, North Vietnamese and South Vietnamese forces stopped fighting. The next several months included the long-awaited return of American PoWs, and the sweeping of mines from the various North Vietnamese waterways that had been dropped from May 1972 onwards.

The following two years saw an uneasy peace as the struggling South Vietnamese government, now devoid of much of the physical presence of American support, balanced precariously between independence and the inevitable resurgence of Communist activity. Neighbouring Cambodia and Laos were in constant turmoil, and by early 1975 the Cambodian capital, Phnom Penh, was lost.

The Communists pushed on into South Vietnam and drove toward Saigon. There was little America could do to prevent the take-over, and the US turned its attention to withdrawing its people and a portion of the South Vietnamese who had worked for American interests during the war.

Task Force 77 and its ships steamed off Saigon, sending helicopters into the beleaguered city. *Hancock* and *Coral Sea* – along with *Enterprise* and *Midway* – launched protective missions to monitor and CAP the Marine and Navy 'helos' as they swooped in and out with their human cargoes.

The smaller carriers' VFP dets occasionally flew recce missions, but it was clear their work was done. A month later, *Coral Sea*'s RF-8Gs covered the unexpected confrontation between Cambodian and American units during the *Mayaguez* Incident, but it was an anti-climactic end to the photo-bird's stellar career.

RF-8Gs continued serving until June 1982, when VFP-63 decommissioned, leaving the Navy without a viable tactical reconnaissance aircraft for the first time in nearly 40 years. The highly touted F-14 TARPS (tactical aerial reconnaissance pod system) fell far short of expectations, especially during its ultimate test in the 1991 Persian Gulf War. And the somewhat intangibles of pride and morale were lacking in the Tomcat crews that tried their hand at reconnaissance.

The photo-Crusader enjoyed a full career in the Naval Air Reserve from 1970 to 1987, equipping two squadrons at Naval Air Facility, Washington, D.C. VFP-206 and -306 carried on the traditions of the fleet photos, initially attracting many former fleet Crusader drivers, both fighter and photo, as well as many younger aviators who were anxious to add Crusader time to their logbooks. But the Crusader, in its reconnaissance

variant, finally retired from service in March 1987, leaving behind an impressive record in peace and war, made all the more so considering how few squadrons flew the RF-8.

Indeed, from 1968 onwards, only VFP-63 retained the RF-8G as its primary equipment. Of 1261 Crusaders produced, 144 were photo-Crusaders, 73 of which were remanufactured as RF-8Gs. Some 20 RF-8s were lost in combat, all in Vietnam, with another 14 lost in operational – non-combat – mishaps. No RF-8s were lost to North Vietnamese MiGs, and all losses were Navy aircraft, the Marine Corps' VMCJ-1 failing to lose any RF-8As – the only model it flew in combat (only reserve squadron VMJ-4 flew 'Golfs' at all) – although several Marine Corps aircraft were damaged by flak. Five VFP-63 aviators were killed in combat, with one missing in action. Six more became PoWs, with one, Lt Charles Klusmann, eventually escaping after three months.

The photo-Crusader, unlike other dedicated reconnaissance aircraft (with the possible exception of the RA-5C Vigilante), created a need and product, as well as a myth, that grew, developed, matured and died within a short, but intense, 20-year career. The RF-8 enjoyed a career way out of proportion with its production numbers. In an unpopular war, the pilots (supported by their dedicated groundcrews) of the VFP and VMCJ dets flew in every condition, often when their compatriots in other squadrons were grounded for weather or politics. Neither the men or machines were found wanting, even in the most arduous times. The men who flew the RF-8 series were true heroes, and represented the best that naval aviation had to offer. They flew a machine that was right for the job that had to be done at the moment. It's doubtful we will ever see such a righteous combination again in military aviation.

**Now an RF-8G, John Glenn's** *Project Bullet* **RF-8 served aboard** *Oriskany* **in 1972. Here, it is shown flying over Japan's Mount Fuji during the det. The veteran aircraft was lost in December 1972 when it hit the carrier's rounddown during an approach. The pilot, Lt Thomas B Scott, was rescued, but Glenn's record-setter now lies at the bottom of the South China Sea**

# APPENDICES

## APPENDIX A

### GLOSSARY

AAA - Anti-aircraft Artillery

Alpha Strike - A large offensive air strike, involving all the carrier air wing's assets, fighters, attack, refuelling, etc.

BARCAP - Barrier Combat Air Patrol. A fighter patrol between the carrier task force and enemy threat

CAG - Commander Air Group. A somewhat archaic term, as wing designation was changed to CVW, and the commander was subsequently referred to as CAW, but CAG remained part of the vocabulary

CAP - Combat Air Patrol

CV - Aircraft carrier. During Vietnam, normal acronym was CVA, designating an attack carrier, where CVS indicated an anti-submarine carrier. In 1975, the Navy dispensed with CVA and CVS, using CV to indicate the carrier's integrated role

CVW - Carrier Air Wing

LSO - Landing Signal Officer

MiGCAP - Standing patrol over the fleet or strike force to protect against any threat from enemy aircraft

OINC - Officer-in-Charge

SAM - Surface-to-Air Missile. A generic term but usually referring to the Soviet-built SA-2 Guideline

SAR - Search and Rescue

TARCAP - Target Combat Air Patrol. Fighters tasked with providing escort protection for the strike force

Trap - An arrested landing aboard a carrier.

VA - Navy Light Attack Squadron

VF - Navy Fighter Squadron

VFP - Navy Light Photographic Squadron

VMCJ - Marine Composite Reconnaissance Squadron

VMF - Marine Fighter Squadron. (AW) was added in 1967 to denote all-weather capability, but was a short-lived designation and was overtaken by VMFA, for fighter and attack

## APPENDIX B

### RF-8A/Gs LOST IN COMBAT

| BuNo | Date | Model | Pilot | Carrier |
|---|---|---|---|---|
| 144611 | 9/4/66 | RF-8A | T Walster* | CVA-19 |
| 144616 | 28/3/68 | RF-8G | M W Wallace* | CVA-14 |
| 144623 | 21/9/67 | RF-8G | M J Vescelius* | CVA-43 |
| 145613 | 16/6/72 | RF-8G | P Ringwood | CVA-41 |
| 145614 | 5/6/67 | RF-8G | C H Haines+ | CVA-31 |
| 145620 | 8/5/65 | RF-8A | W B Wilson | CVA-41 |
| 146823 | 6/6/64 | RF-8A | C Klusmann+ | CVA-63 |
| 146825 | 8/9/65 | RF-8A | R D Rudolph* | CVA-34 |
| 146826 | 8/9/65 | RF-8A | C B Goodwin++ | CVA-43 |
| 146828 | 29/8/65 | RF-8A | H S McWhorter* | CVA-34 |
| 146830 | 21/6/66 | RF-8A | L L Eastman+ | CVA-19 |
| 146831 | 5/5/66 | RF-8A | J Heilig+ | CVA-19 |
| 146843 | 19/4/66 | RF-8A | R F Ball | CVA-14 |
| 146849 | 13/8/65 | RF-8A | P A Manning | CVA-43 |
| 146852 | 1/6/65 | RF-8A | F P Crosby* | CVA-31 |
| 146873 | 22/7/72 | RF-8G | G L Paige+ | CVA-41 |
| 146874 | 31/8/66 | RF-8G | T A Tucker | CVA-34 |
| 146881 | 1/6/65 | RF-8A | M R Fields | CVA-41 |
| 146886 | 22/5/68 | RF-8G | E F Miller+ | CVA-31 |
| 146889 | 8/10/66 | RF-8A | F D Litvin | CVA-43 |

**Key**
* Killed in action   ++ Missing in action   + Prisoner of war

# APPENDIX C

## VFP AND VMCJ SQUADRON DEPLOYMENTS IN VIETNAM

| Squadron/Air Wing | Model | Carrier | Tail Code and Modex | Dates |
|---|---|---|---|---|
| **VFP-62 'Fightin' Photos'** | | | | |
| VFP-62 Det 42/CVW-1 | RF-8G | *Franklin D Roosevelt* | AB 9xx | 21 Jun 66 to 1 Feb 67 |
| **VFP-63 'Eyes of the Fleet'** | | | | |
| VFP-63 Det C/CVW-11 | RF-8A | *Kitty Hawk* | PP 91x | 17 Oct 63 to 20 Jul 64 |
| VFP-63 Det E/CVW-19 | RF-8A | *Bon Homme Richard* | PP 9xx | 28 Jan 64 to 21 Nov 64 |
| VFP-63 Det B/CVW-5 | RF-8A | *Ticonderoga* | PP 93x | 14 Apr 64 to 15 Dec 64 |
| VFP-63 Det F/CVW-14 | RF-8A | *Constellation* | PP 3xx | 5 May 64 to 1 Feb 65 |
| VFP-63 Det M/CVW-9 | RF-8A | *Ranger* | PP 9xx | 5 Aug 64 to 6 May 65 |
| VFP-63 Det L/CVW-21 | RF-8A | *Hancock* | PP 9xx | 21 Oct 64 to 29 May 65 |
| VFP-63 Det D/CVW-15 | RF-8A | *Coral Sea* | PP 9xx | 7 Dec 64 to 1 Nov 65 |
| VFP-63 Det A/CVW-2 | RF-8A | *Midway* | PP 9xx | 6 Mar 65 to 23 Nov 65 |
| VFP-63 Det G/CVW-16 | RF-8A | *Oriskany* | PP 9xx | 5 Apr 65 to 16 Dec 65 |
| VFP-63 Det E/CVW-19 | RF-8A | *Bon Homme Richard* | PP 9xx | 21 Apr 65 to 13 Jan 66 |
| VFP-63 Det B/CVW-14 | RF-8A | *Ticonderoga* | PP 93x | 28 Sep 65 to 13 May 66 |
| VFP-63 Det L/CVW-21 | RF-8A | *Hancock* | PP 90x | 10 Nov 65 to 1 Aug 66 |
| VFP-63 Det G/CVW-16 | RF-8A | *Oriskany* | AH 6xx | 26 May 66 to 16 Nov 66 |
| VFP-63 Det A/CVW-2 | RF-8G | *Coral Sea* | PP 89x | 29 Jul 66 to 23 Feb 67 |
| VFP-63 Det E/CVW-19 | RF-8G | *Ticonderoga* | PP 91x | 15 Oct 66 to 29 May 67 |
| VFP-63 Det B/CVW-5 | RF-8G | *Hancock* | PP 91x | 5 Jan 67 to 22 Jul 67 |
| VFP-63 Det L/CVW-21 | RF-8G | *Bon Homme Richard* | PP 9xx | 26 Jan 67 to 25 Aug 67 |
| VFP-63 Det 11/CVW-10 | RF-8G | *Intrepid* | AK 4xx | 11 May 67 to 30 Dec 67 |
| VFP-63 Det 34/CVW-16 | RF-8G | *Oriskany* | AH 6xx | 16 Jul 67 to 31 Jan 68 |
| VFP-63 Det 43/CVW-15 | RF-8G | *Coral Sea* | NL 71x | 26 July 67 to 6 Apr 68 |
| VFP-63 Det 14/CVW-19 | RF-8G | *Ticonderoga* | NM 6xx | 27 Dec 67 to 17 Aug 68 |
| VFP-63 Det 31/CVW-5 | RF-8G | *Bon Homme Richard* | NF 60x | 27 Jan 68 to 10 Oct 68 |
| VFP-63 Det 11/CVW-10 | RF-8G | *Intrepid* | AK 4xx | 4 Jun 68 to 8 Feb 69 |
| VFP-63 Det 19/CVW-21 | RF-8G | *Hancock* | NP 6xx | 18 Jul 68 to 3 Mar 69 |
| VFP-63 Det 43/CVW-15 | RF-8G | *Coral Sea* | NL 5xx | 7 Sep 68 to 18 Apr 69 |
| VFP-63 Det 14/CVW-16 | RF-8G | *Ticonderoga* | AH 60x | 1 Feb 69 to 18 Sep 69 |
| VFP-63 Det 31/CVW-5 | RF-8G | *Bon Homme Richard* | NF 60x | 18 Mar 69 to 29 Oct 69 |
| VFP-63 Det 34/CVW-19 | RF-8G | *Oriskany* | NM 6xx | 16 Apr 69 to 17 Nov 69 |
| VFP-63 Det 19/CVW-21 | RF-8G | *Hancock* | NP 60x | 2 Aug 69 to 15 Apr 70 |
| VFP-63 Det 43/CVW-15 | RF-8G | *Coral Sea* | NL 60x | 23 Sep 69 to 1 Jul 70 |
| VFP-63 Det 38/CVW-10 | RF-8G | *Shangri-la* | AJ 6xx | 5 Mar 70 to 17 Dec 70 |
| VFP-63 Det 31/CVW-5 | RF-8G | *Bon Homme Richard* | NF 60x | 2 Apr 70 to 12 Nov 70 |
| VFP-63 Det 34/CVW-19 | RF-8G | *Oriskany* | NM 6xx | 14 May 70 to 10 Dec 70 |
| VFP-63 Det 1/CVW-21 | RF-8G | *Hancock* | NP 60x | 22 Oct 70 to 2 Jun 71 |
| VFP-63 Det 3/CVW-5 | RF-8G | *Midway* | NF 60x | 16 Apr 71 to 6 Nov 71 |
| VFP-63 Det 4/CVW-19 | RF-8G | *Oriskany* | NM 60x | 14 May 71 to 18 Dec 71 |
| VFP-63 Det 5/CVW-15 | RF-8G | *Coral Sea* | NL 60x | 12 Nov 71 to 17 Jul 72 |
| VFP-63 Det 1/CVW-21 | RF-8G | *Hancock* | NP 60x | 7 Jan 72 to 3 Oct 72 |
| VFP-63 Det 3/CVW-5 | RF-8G | *Midway* | NF 60x | 10 Apr 72 to 3 Mar 73 |
| VFP-63 Det 4/CVW-19 | RF-8G | *Oriskany* | NM 60x | 5 Jun 72 to 30 Mar 73 |
| VFP-63 Det 5/CVW-15 | RF-8G | *Coral Sea* | NL 60x | 9 Mar 73 to 8 Nov 73 |
| VFP-63 Det 1/CVW-21 | RF-8G | *Hancock* | NP 6xx | 8 May 73 to 8 Jan 74 |

| Squadron/Air Wing | Model | Carrier | Tail Code and Modex | Dates |
|---|---|---|---|---|
| **VMCJ-1 Golden Hawks*** | | | | |
| VMCJ-1 | RF-8A | *Kitty Hawk* | RM 1x | May to Jun 64 |
| VMCJ-1 | RF-8A | *Ticonderoga* | RM 1x | Dec 64 |
| VMCJ-1 | RF-8A | *Bon Homme Richard* | RM 1x | Dec 64 |
| VMCJ-1 | RF-8A | *Constellation* | RM 1x | Sep 64 |
| VMCJ-1 | RF-8A | *Coral Sea* | RM 1x | Feb 65 |
| VMCJ-1 | RF-8A | *Oriskany* | RM 1x | Jun 65 |

**Notes**

* VMCJ-1 dets were not aboard a specific carrier for the entire deployment. Months noted were during heaviest activity during cruise. Besides its carrier detachments of 1964-65, VMCJ-1 flew RF-8As from Da Nang, SVn, from 1964 to 1967. The composite squadron also operated the EF-10 ELINT-gatherer, which was a development of the Korean War's twin-jet F3D Skyknight nightfighter. The EF-10 served until 1969 when it was replaced by the Grumman EA-6A. The RF-8A's replacement, the RF-4B Phantom II, had arrived beginning in 1966. Like the F-8 squadrons, the VMCJ-1 dets used the same aircraft, simply rotating them around the incoming groups as the retiring members finished their tours. Thus, the aircraft were soon tired and worn out from the stresses of combat by the end of 1967.

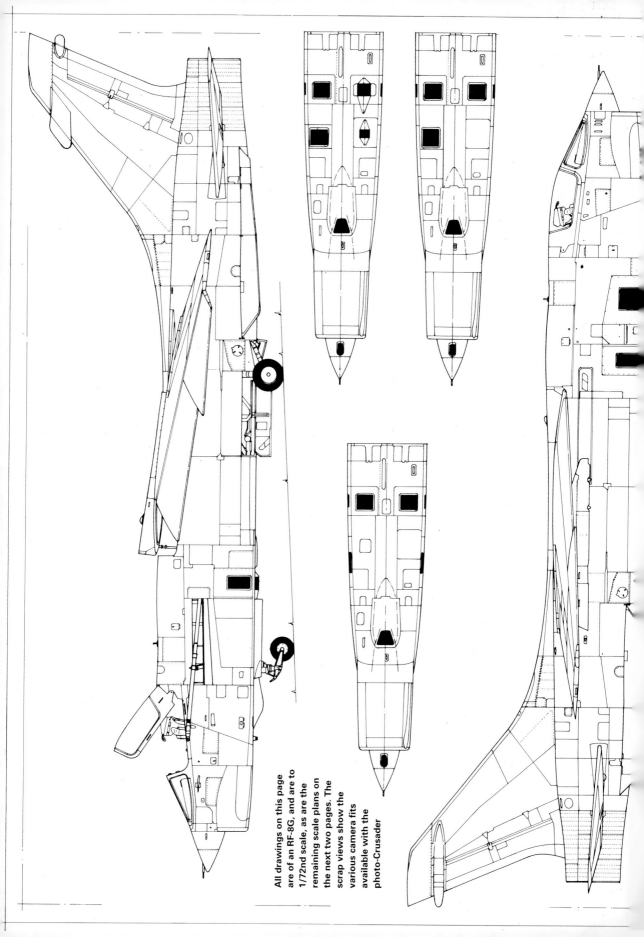

All drawings on this page are of an RF-8G, and are to 1/72nd scale, as are the remaining scale plans on the next two pages. The scrap views show the various camera fits available with the photo-Crusader

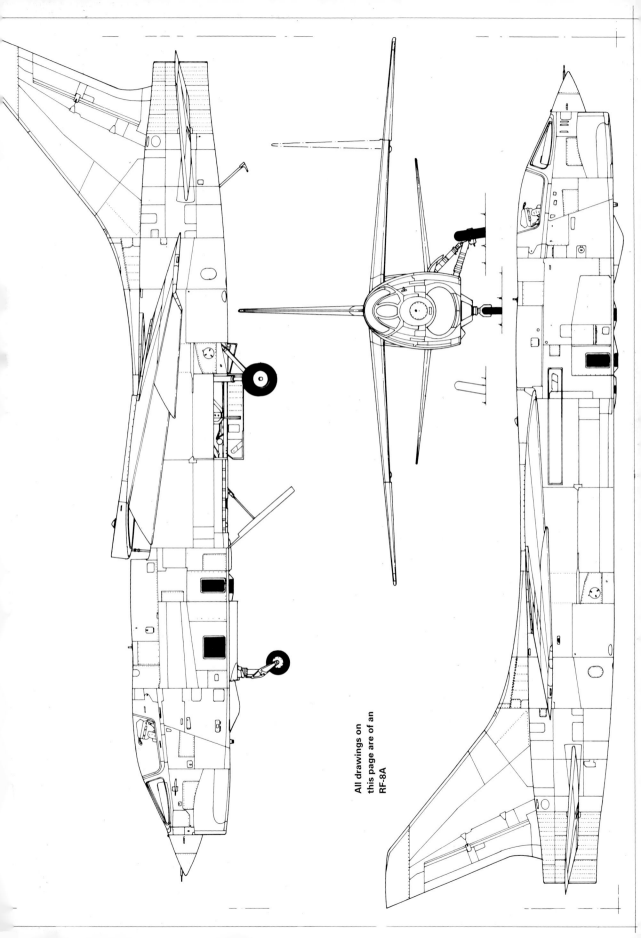

All drawings on
this page are of an
RF-8A

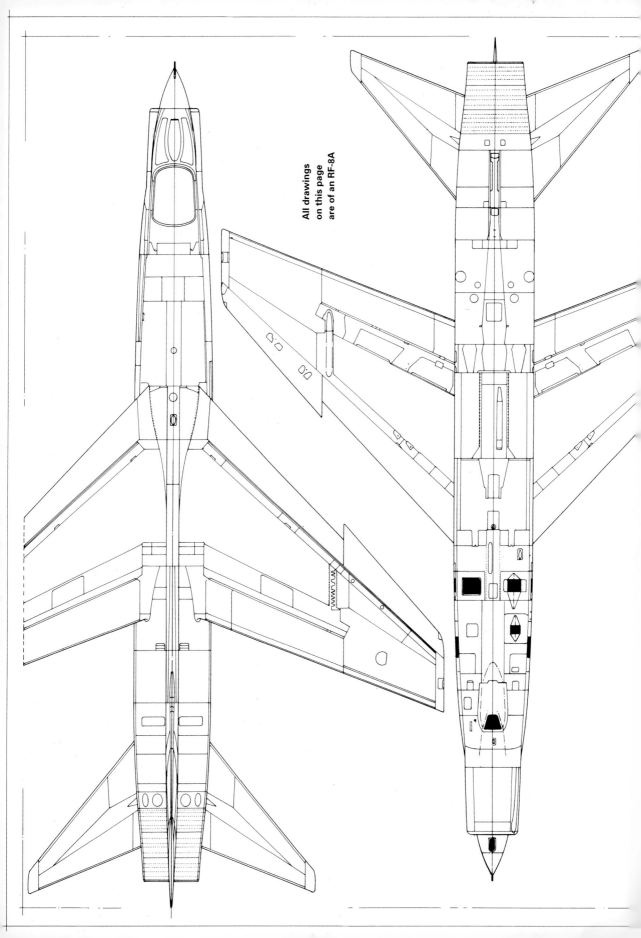

All drawings
on this page
are of an RF-8A

# COLOUR PLATES

## 1

**RF-8A BuNo 146863 CY 11 of VMCJ-2 ('Gitmo' Det), NAF Guántanamo, Cuba, October 1962**

BuNo 146863 was one of a small number of photo-birds used to overfly Cuba from the US Navy's forward base on the island itself. Note the unit's famous *Playboy Bunny* emblem below the wing leading edge. This aircraft was upgraded to RF-8G specs several years later, and subsequently survived many years of service with VFP-63 until being finally retired (as PP 646) to the 'desert boneyard' at Davis-Monthan AFB, in Arizona, on 15 December 1980 – it is still part of the Aerospace Maintenance and Regeneration Center (AMARC) inventory today.

## 2

**RF-8A BuNo 145646 CY 1 (also CY 5 later on) of VMCJ-2 ('Gitmo' Det), NAF Guántanamo, Cuba, October 1962**

This aircraft bears the name 'LTCOL W.E.DOMINA' immediately below its windscreen. Note the black *Bunny* insignia this time applied above the CY tailcode. Although *Playboy* magazine refused permission to use its well-known logo as shown in each issue, an understanding representative from the publication suggested bending one ear to distance it from the 'official' insignia. Photos of the unit's aircraft at the time show that although not always carried by VMCJ-2 Crusaders, the 'bunny' motif occasionally lacked a 'bent-ear' when it was displayed, and then, only on the starboard side of the fuselage. This particular aircraft was lost as an RF-8G whilst serving with VFP-63 Det 2 during pre-cruise work-ups aboard *Coral Sea* on 13 October 1979.

## 3

**RF-8A BuNo 146886 GA 906 of VFP-62, NAS Key West, November 1962**

Bearing the name 'W.F.FOARD' on its starboard canopy rail, this aircraft also boasts various unofficial unit insignia, including a blue-and-gold knight's helmet, a sword and shield and a small *Playboy* rabbit (a nod to the Marines of VMCJ-2) just below the number '9' in the nose modex. This aircraft was later upgraded into an RF-8G and shot down by AAA on 22 May 1968 while serving with VFP-63's det in CVA-31 – its pilot on this occasion, Lt(jg) E F Miller, was captured and became a PoW.

## 4

**RF-8A BuNo 146871 GA 910 flown by Cdr William Ecker, CO of VFP-62, NAS Key West, late November 1962**

VFP-62's CO, Cdr William Ecker, flew this aircraft on a number of his missions over Cuba during the crisis. The Navy unit commendation ribbon painted on the nose of the Crusader dates this scheme as late November 1962, VFP-62 having been personally presented with the award (the first issued during peacetime) by President John F Kennedy during the latter's visit to Key West on the 26th of that month. Like many of the Cuban Crisis RF-8As, this aircraft was later remanufactured as a G-model and saw heavy action in Vietnam with the VFP-63 det on board *Oriskany* in 1966. It was finally lost in an operational accident whilst flying with VFP-63 on 2 December 1976.

## 5

**RF-8A BuNo 146823 PP 920 flown by Lt Charles Klusmann, VFP-63 Det C, USS *Kitty Hawk*, June 1964**

This was the aircraft flown by Lt Charles Klusmann when he was shot down by flak near the village of Ban Ban, on the Plaine des Jarres, on 6 June 1964. The destruction of BuNo 146823 marked the Crusader's first loss in combat.

## 6

**RF-8A BuNo 145639 RM 18 of VMCJ-1 aboard USS *Kitty Hawk*, May/June 1964**

Part of the joint Navy/Marine Corps dets of 1964-65, this aircraft retains its distinctive VMCJ-1 arrowhead marking and RM codes on the fin, as well as the non-standard USMC two-digit nose modex.

## 7

**RF-8A BuNo 146866 RM 17 flown by 1Lt Denis Kiely of VMCJ-1 aboard USS *Kitty Hawk*, May/June 1964**

This aircraft was flown over Vietnam on a number of occasions by original VMCJ-1 det member 1Lt Denis Kiely during the early weeks of the escalating conflict in South-East Asia. Later converted into an RF-8G, BuNo 146866 was lost in an operational accident in the USA whilst serving with VFP-63 on 31 July 1970.

## 8

**RF-8A BuNo 146838 RM 11 flown by 1Lt Denis Kiely of VMCJ-1 aboard USS *Kitty Hawk*, May/June 1964**

Almost identical in appearance to the previous profile, this RF-8A was also used by 1Lt Denis Kiely to overfly a number of Vietnamese 'hot spots' during the summer of 1964. Unlike BuNo 146866, this aircraft survived the conflict in South-East Asia (and a wheels-up landing as AH 601 during VFP-63 Det 14's work-ups for *Ticonderoga*'s TF 77 deployment in 1969) and went on to enjoy a frontline career with VFP-63 that lasted until it was retired to Davis-Monthan (as PP 644) on 17 December 1981, where it remains to this day.

## 9

**RF-8A BuNo 146892 RM 10 of VMCJ-1 at Da Nang, 1964-65**

VMCJ-1's photo-birds wore a standard scheme (although this RF-8A differs from the previous

VMCJ-1 aircraft seen in profile by having its air system exhaust heat shield painted black) both at sea aboard TF 77 carriers and on land at the sprawling Marine Air base at Da Nang, in South Vietnam. This aircraft was later written off whilst flying as an RF-8G with VFP-63 on 15 July 1976 – indeed, it was one of eight RF-8s lost by the unit in a 'black' 14-month spell between 1 June 1976 and 30 August 1977 that almost resulted in the unit being prematurely disbanded. However, the tactical value of the ageing photo-bird to the Seventh Fleet, in particular, kept the squadron alive, just, and improved spares supply and selective recruiting for key maintenance areas turned the accident rate around. As a result of these changes, only three jets were lost from the end of August 1977 until the unit disestablished on 30 June 1982.

## 10
### RF-8A BuNo 146855 PP 908 of VFP-63 Det F aboard USS *Constellation*, 1964
This aircraft was a veteran of many *Team Yankee* sorties from the deck of CVA-64 during the carrier's 68 days on the line between August and November 1964. Later upgraded to RF-8G specs, BuNo 146855 earned the dubious distinction of being the last Crusader to crash in Navy service when its pilot, reservist Cdr David Strong (XO of VFP-206), was forced to eject soon after taking off from NAS Miramar on 11 March 1985. Part of a two-aircraft flight participating in an ACDUTRA (ACtive DUty for TRAining) period on the West Coast, Strong had successfully launched in AF 606 but then heard an explosion and suffered immediate power loss as soon as he had come out of afterburner. He stayed with his aircraft as long as he could in order to ensure that it did not crash into a nearby office park, and once clear of danger, Strong successfully ejected at just 250 ft above the ground – despite being outside of the seat's envelope. He was later awarded a rare peacetime DFC for remaining in BuNo 146855 beyond the limits required in order to keep the stricken jet away from a heavily populated area.

## 11
### RF-8A BuNo 145632 PP 967 of VFP-63 Det A aboard USS *Midway*, 1965
Illustrating VFP-63's affinity for decorating their jets with caricature's of animals, this RF-8A has an alligator sprayed onto its fin above the PP code. Assigned to CVW-2 during CVA-41's 1965 TF 77 cruise, Det A lost two RF-8As just 24 days apart to North Vietnamese AAA in May-June 1965, although both pilots were recovered. BuNo 145632, meanwhile, survived long enough to be upgraded to an RF-8G, but it too was lost when it crashed off the Philippines on 1 December 1969.

## 12
### RF-8A BuNo 144616 PP 934 of VFP-63 Det B aboard USS *Ticonderoga*, 1965
Again wearing typical VFP-63 codes and detail markings, this RF-8A also boasts an animal motif (it

appears to be a squirrel) above its PP codes. This aircraft fell victim to enemy AAA during *Ticonderoga*'s next TF 77 deployment when it was struck by small arms fire over Laos on 28 March 1968, its pilot, Lt Cdr M W Wallace, being killed in the resulting crash.

## 13
### RF-8G BuNo 144624 AB 902 of VFP-62 Det 42 aboard USS *Franklin D Roosevelt*, June 1966
BuNo 144624 briefly participated in the sole TF 77 deployment of CVA-42 as part of VFP-62's Det 42 – the *FDR* cruise was also VFP-62's only taste of combat over Vietnam. Just 43 days after arriving on the line, AB 902 was lost in an operational mishap on 6 September 1966 which resulted in the death of its pilot. BuNo 144624 was the sole casualty of Det 42's 95 days of near-continuous combat.

## 14
### RF-8G BuNo 146122 AH 603 flown by Lt Andre Coltrin of VFP-63 Det G aboard USS *Oriskany*, June-November 1966
This aircraft was flown on numerous occasions by Lt Andre Coltrin from the compact deck of *Oriskany* during 87 days on the line. Note the total absence of distinguishing markings aside from the 'VFP-63' titling – even the unit's common PP tailcode has been replaced by CVW-16's distinctive stylised AH code, which was the first time this had happened to a VFP-63 photo det aboard a TF 77 carrier.

## 15
### RF-8G BuNo 146871 AH 601 of VFP-63 Det G aboard USS *Oriskany*, June-November 1966
The subject of profile two, this jet is depicted here almost four years later carrying the name 'LCDR TOM TUCKER' on its canopy rails. This pilot had the unenviable distinction of being the only Det G pilot to be shot down during the cruise. He was hit by AAA whilst flying BuNo 146874 ('Corktip 602') on 31 August 1966, but was quickly rescued from the sea, and the clutches of the North Vietnamese, by an SH-3A from HS-6 aboard USS *Kearsarge*.

## 16
### RF-8G BuNo 146848 PP 916 flown by Lt(jg) Leonard E Johnson of VFP-63 Det B aboard USS *Hancock*, January-July 1967
Wearing VFP-63's traditional star-spangled dark blue fin and wingtip bands, PP tailcode (repeated on the upper surface of the starboard wing) and helmeted *Snoopy* drawing, this jet was regularly flown by Lt(jg) Leonard E Johnson during *Hancock*'s sole war cruise with CVW-5 embarked – the remaining seven cruises completed by this ship were with CVW-21. This particular aircraft was the third of eight lost by VFP-63 between June 1976 and August 1977, the photo-bird being destroyed on 12 August 1976.

## 17
### RF-8G BuNo 145645 PP 907 of VFP-63 Det B aboard USS *Hancock*, 1967

No det-inspired markings on this plain RF-8G aboard CVA-19 for the carrier's third combat tour of the Vietnam war. Det B came through 102 days on the line totally unscathed, failing to lose a single RF-8 either in combat or on routine operations – in stark contrast to Det L's experience aboard *Hancock* exactly a year earlier, when three RF-8As were lost to North Vietnamese AAA, leaving a pilot dead and two as PoWs. BuNo 145645 currently resides at Davis-Monthan, having been retired to Arizona by VFP-63 on 12 May 1982. BuNo 145645 is also the subject of profile 28.

## 18

**RF-8G BuNo 145633 NL 712 flown by Lt(jg) Jay Miller of VFP-63 Det 43 aboard USS *Coral Sea*, September 1967**

A regular entry in Lt(jg) Jay Miller's flight log during his *Coral Sea* cruise, this aircraft carries the familiar VFP-63 bands, plus the infrequently seen det insignia, atop the fin. Note also the CVW-15 NL codes and rare tail ECM fairing forward of the fin band. This particular aircraft survived to see the very end of the RF-8's long naval career, being amongst the last three photo-Crusaders retired by reservists VFP-206 at NAF Washington, D.C., Andrews AFB, on 26 March 1987. It is currently one of 17 RF-8Gs stored in the AMARC facility presumably awaiting the scrapper's torch.

## 19

**RF-8G BuNo 144618 NL 710 flown by Lt(jg) Will Gray of VFP-63 Det 43 aboard USS *Coral Sea*, September 1967**

Although rather more weather-beaten than NL 712, this RF-8G bears identical markings as befits a 'det mate' embarked in CVA-43 for the carrier's 'bloody' 1967-68 combat cruise that lasted 132 days on the line. This aircraft was regularly flown by Lt(jg) Will Gray throughout the deployment, and carries his name on the canopy rail – it also has the ECM fairing affixed to the fin leading edge. BuNo 144618 is also a survivor, having been present at Davis-Monthan since its retirement from VFP-63 on 15 April 1982.

## 20

**RF-8G BuNo 145639 NL 713 of VFP-63 Det 43 aboard USS *Coral Sea*, 1968**

Aside from the standard blue fin and wing-tip bands, this aircraft also has a missile-riding *Wile E. Coyote* caricature (of *Road Runner* cartoon fame) painted just below the NL tailcode.

## 21

**RF-8G BuNo 145636 NM 603 of VFP-63 Det 4 aboard USS *Oriskany*, 1971**

By 1971-72, a number of VFP-63 dets had adopted black tail, wing-tip and ventral strake bands for their aircraft in place of the dark blue of the 1960s. A veteran of several previous TF 77 cruises, this jet enjoyed a relatively quiet time during *Oriskany's* 1971 deployment, which saw the carrier on the line for 75 days in total. This cruise was to be BuNo

145636's last with TF 77, for it was lost on a routine flight back in the USA on 1 August 1972.

## 22

**RF-8G BuNo 146845 NP 603 of VFP-63 Det 1 aboard USS *Hancock*, 1971**

When Det 1 embarked in *Hancock* for the carrier's 1970-71 deployment, it emulated its predecessor aboard the vessel – Det 19 – by foregoing VFP-63's traditional black or blue 'star-spangled' bands for the red-and-white checkerboard and red chevron tail markings of the embarked fighter units, VF-24 and -211. The RF-8Gs also boasted checkerboard wing-tip bands, although these were not present on CVW-21's F-8Js. This particular aircraft was further embellished with a rare nickname – *FLYING SQUIRL* – just above the national marking, although the relevance of this sobriquet is unknown. BuNo 146845 was amongst the last RF-8Gs retired to Davis-Monthan by VFP-306, the jet arriving in Arizona (as ND 604) on 25 September 1984 – just five days prior to the reserve unit's decommissioning at NAF Washington D.C.

## 23

**RF-8G BuNo 146863 NF 602 flown by Capt Jim Morgan, USAF, of VFP-63 Det 3 aboard USS *Midway*, 1971**

Seen as an RF-8A in profile three, this jet was upgraded to RF-8G specs and sent on a number of TF 77 deployments during the Vietnam conflict. Whilst embarked on CVA-41, the aircraft was assigned to USAF RF-4C exchange pilot Capt Jim Morgan. Evidently a good 'stick', Morgan enjoyed his tour with the Navy light-photo squadron.

## 24

**RF-8G BuNo 146892 NP 612 of VFP-63 Det 1 aboard USS *Hancock*, 1972**

When compared with the Det 1 RF-8 featured in profile 22, this aircraft boasts a scheme that better reflects VFP-63's more traditional markings. The garish checkerboard (both on the fin and wing-tips) has been replaced with stars, although the primary colour remains 'fighter red' and a more emaciated rendition of VF-24's 'tick' is still very much in evidence on the fin. No photo-birds were lost in combat during 165 days on the line (this was *Hancock's* longest period in action during her record eight TF 77 deployments), although an RF-8G (BuNo 146861) was lost in a non-fatal operational crash on 5 September 1972 during CVA-19's final 19 days on the line – F-8J BuNo 150229 from VF-24 was also lost during a non-combat sortie on this day, although again its pilot was recovered. BuNo 146892 later became the second of eight VFP-63 jets lost in 1976-77, crashing on 15 July 1976.

## 25

**RF-8G BuNo 146876 PP 901 of Cdr J M Schulze, Commander of VFP-63, NAS Miramar, 1972**

This aircraft is unusual in having the double fin bands and ventral fin marking applied in blue rather than black. Being shore-based at the time, it also wears VFP-63's traditional PP tail codes. Finally, as the aircraft assigned to the unit's colourful commanding officer, Cdr J M Schulze (see figure plates), the RF-8 carries the '01' modex, prefixed by VFP-63's familiar number '9'. BuNo 146876 was the first photo-bird lost by VFP-63 during its 'black' spell in 1976-77, the jet crashing on 1 June 1976.

### 26
### RF-8G BuNo 144608 NM 601 of VFP-63 Det 4 aboard USS *Oriskany*, June 1972 to January 1973

BuNo 144608 had gained considerable fame some 15 years before CVA-34's 1972-73 TF 77 deployment as the mount for Maj John Glenn's record-breaking *Project Bullet* coast-to-coast flight across America on 16 July 1957. Only the third photo-Crusader built (then designated an F8U-1P), BuNo 144608 was later remanufactured as an RF-8G after a number of years of fleet service as a redesignated RF-8A. It was finally destroyed on 13 December 1972 when its pilot, Lt Thomas B Scott, struck *Oriskany*'s deck short of the arresting wires whilst attempting to land back aboard the carrier at the end of a reconnaissance training mission over the South China Sea. The pilot safely ejected.

### 27
### RF-8G BuNo 146856 NF 601 flown by Lt Cdr Will Gray, OINC of VFP-63's Det 3 aboard USS *Midway* in December 1973

This RF-8G, which was assigned to det commander Lt Cdr Will Gray, also carries a small green *Snoopy* atop the 'F' in CVW-5's NF code. BuNo 146856 was retired to Davis-Monthan on 17 July 1981 by VFP-63, and after almost six years in Arizona it was moved to NAS North Island, California, on 10 February 1987.

### 28
### RF-8G BuNo 145645 NF 601 flown by Lt Cdr Will Gray of VFP-63 Det 3 aboard USS *Midway*, 1974

In stark contrast to the colourful scheme adopted by Det 3 on it previous TF 77 cruise just 12 months earlier, the only distinguishing marking on this photo-Crusader is the traditional green *Snoopy* caricature atop the 'F' in the tailcode. This particular aircraft also boasts a larger forward camera window which actually obscures part of the 'star and bar'. Carrying the titling 'LCDR WILL GRAY' on its canopy rails, this is the third aircraft featured within this profile section to be flown by one of the photo-recce community's most successful pilots. Gray eventually retired as a captain after a varied career that had seen him command a Prowler squadron after leaving VFP-63, as well as later serving as a naval attaché in Asia. BuNo 145645 is also the subject of profile 17.

### 29
### RF-8G BuNo 146835 NL 603 of VFP-63 Det 5 aboard USS *Coral Sea*, 1974

Unlike CVA-41's Det 3, which was operating with TF 77 at the same time in the crowded waters of the South China Sea, Det 5 (aboard *Midway*'s sister-ship) not only retained VFP-63's traditional dark blue fin band, but also adorned the ventral strakes of their aircraft in a matching blue shade, detailed with a white sword. This unique scheme was worn by the jets of CVA-43's photo-det during the over-seeing of the withdrawal of US nationals from South Vietnam in April 1975 and the *Mayaguez* Incident the following month – both incidents in which *Coral Sea* played an active role. BuNo 146835 sub-sequently survived another seven years of fleet service with VFP-63 until retired to Davis-Monthan on 18 May 1982, where it still resides today.

## FIGURE PLATES

### 1
Cdr William Ecker, CO of VFP-62 during the Cuban missile crisis in October/November 1962. He is wearing a standard issue one-piece khaki flying suit, over which he has strapped on an SV-2 survival vest, MA-2 torso harness and W/Mk-3C waist life-preserver. Ecker has also donned a bandoleer of bullets (for his side-arm) over his flight suit, which passes over his right shoulder and under his left armpit. He is holding his large APH-6 flight helmet, APH standing for Aviator's Protective Helmet – note its stylised paint scheme which, appropriately, resembles a roll of film. Finally, Ecker's footwear consists of regulation issue aviator's steel-toed, brown flight boots.

### 2
Capt Harold 'Hoss' Austin of VMCJ-2's 'Gitmo Det' at Guántanamo Bay, in Cuba, in October/November 1962. Like Ecker, he is wearing a one-piece khaki flying suit devoid of any personal or unit patches. A member of the forgotten Marine Corps photo det at 'Gitmo', Austin has a staff sergeant's metal rank pin affixed to his left suit collar, signifying that he was technically an NCO (pay grade E-5) fast jet pilot in Cuba for a single day until his commission as a captain was cleared. Austin was originally an enlisted Marine, and this odd situation arose because of the implementation of a new commissioning programme which cleared away so-called 'temporary officer' ranks in the Corps at the time. Tucked into Austin's green nylon combat webbing is a brown rawhide-handled, sheathed knife, which was considered by many to be a key survival tool. Austin's final item of flying gear is a pair of well-worn fawn-coloured gloves.

### 3
Capt John I Hudson of VMCJ-2, temporarily assigned to VFP-62 during the Cuban missile crisis of October/November 1962. Like Cdr Ecker, he is wearing a standard issue one-piece khaki flying suit, over which he has strapped on an SV-2 sur-vival vest, MA-2 torso harness and W/Mk-3C waist life-preserver. Note the issue angled flashlight hanging tucked into the top of his SV-2 survival vest. As with Ecker and Austin, Hudson's footwear

comprises regulation issue aviator's steel-toed, brown flight boots.

**4**

Lt Charles Klusmann of VFP-63 at NAS Miramar in early 1965. Again attired in a standard-issue khaki flight suit, SV-2 survival vest, MA-2 torso harness, W/Mk-3C waist life-preserver and Mk-2 anti-gravity (G-suit), the details of Klusmann's battery-powered emergency rescue strobe light are particularly visible on his right shoulder. The pilot's two leg-restraint garters above and below the knees can also be seen, these being a feature of the Martin-Baker seats used in the Vietnam-period F-8 and F-4. The white or blue colouring of these straps signified where the individual garter went. One of the first things a pilot did after positioning himself in his ejection seat – before connecting his four harness fittings to the seat – was to thread a long cloth-covered cable through the four restraints and plug the cable into the opposite, lower portion, of the metal seat. If he had to eject, and a split-second before the seat began moving up the rails, the cable pulled the pilot's legs tight against the seat to prevent them from flailing during the ejection. Other details on his flight gear include the rocket-jet fittings on his shoulder straps and the V-ring helicopter hoist connection, the chest-mounted strap that could be pulled to tighten the fit of his survival vest, a large survival knife pocketed in his G-suit on the outside of his left leg and the unprotected pens on his left sleeve. This was the style for many years, all aviators carrying their writing implements in this fashion despite the acknowledged fact that they constituted a major FOD hazard. By the 1980s, a flap was sewn (typically at unit level) over the pen pocket to keep them from falling out in the cockpit. Note Klusmann's brown high-top brown flight boots and his large APH-6 flight helmet adorned with *NAVY* titling in a style which proved popular in VFP-63 during this period.

**5**

Lt Cdr J M Schulze, OINC VFP-63 Det B aboard USS *Hancock* in the South China Sea in 1967. The first regulation issue jungle-green flight suits began to appear in fleet squadrons in mid-1966, these having been deemed to offer a downed aviator a better chance of camouflaging himself effectively amongst his tropical surroundings in the event of him ejecting 'up north'. Over his tight-fitting suit, Schulze has strapped, buttoned and zippered on his Mk-3C survival vest, regulation Mk-2 anti-gravity (G-suit) and parachute harness, plus secured his trusty jungle knife in a handy mid-chest position. His gloves are also of a more modern issue, being finished in nylon with Velcro patches at the wrists. Finally, Schulze has donned his well-known Prussian spiked helmet, which he would frequently wear right up to the point of pulling the canopy shut on his jet!

**6**

Lt Cdr Tom Tucker, OINC VFP-63 Det G, NAS Miramar, early 1966. The International Orange flight suit was traditionally worn by all naval aviators when flying either from shore bases in the USA or from carrier decks during pre-cruise work-ups. Because of its colouring, the suit offered its wearer a better chance of being spotted either in the water or on land in the event of an ejection. Tucker is wearing a highly-prized MA-1 nylon flight jacket over his suit, rather than the more common brown leather A-1 of World War 2 fame. Although the former was less durable than its leather equivalent, the MA-1 nevertheless became synonymous with frontline naval aviators. Once considered mission ready by the fleet unit, the pilot was then presented with a squadron patch to sew onto his MA-1 – Tucker wears the VFP-63 insignia on his right breast. Opposite is his black leather identity tag, with his name, rank and naval aviator wings picked out in gold.

## COLOUR SECTION

**1**

Lt Charles Klusmann indulges in a little self-portraiture during a hop in June 1964. Note the large butterfly release on his flight helmet for his oxygen mask. These rather cumbersome devices were replaced by bayonet fittings that slid into the helmet and locked, and could be pulled out again in one motion. The large yellow-and-black ring behind his head is, of course, the handle for the ejection-seat face curtain

**2**

The scene on the flight deck before a mission from *Kitty Hawk* in June 1964. The Crusader in the foreground is VFP-63 Det C's BuNo 146827 PP 918. Note the pilots' highly decorated flight helmets

**3**

Details of typical aviator flying gear of the mid-1960s are shown in this view of Lt Klusmann climbing into his Crusader. Besides the brown flight boots – black boots did not arrive until 1967 – we can see the two leg-restraint garters above and below the knees and a large survival knife pocketed in his G-suit on the outside of his left leg

**4**

A rare view of RF-8G BuNo 144624 of VFP-62 Det 42 during the Atlantic VFP squadron's only Vietnam cruise in 1966 aboard the *FDR*. Although the squadron did not lose any photo-Crusaders in combat, several were hit by flak and small arms, and one was lost operationally – this very jet, in fact, on 6 September 1966, resulting in the death of its pilot. Shortly after returning from this cruise the squadron decommissioned

**5**

The *Oriskany* photo det in 1966. Wearing a pre-deployment orange flight suit, Andre Coltrin is seen second from left, while the det OINC, Lt Cdr Tom Tucker, is standing second from right. The four pilots flank the non-aviator PI officer, seen in his dress blues.

**6**

An RF-8G gets the launch signal for a September 1967 mission from the *Oriskany*. Note the bridles immediately below the aft-most camera window, which connect the Crusader to the catapult shuttle

**7**

Two RF-8Gs of Det Lima fly astern of USS *Hancock* during the 1967 deployment. *Hancock*'s photo dets sustained some of the worst loss rates of the entire war, although on this particular cruise not a single jet was lost either in combat or operationally. Of the two jets seen here, BuNo 144625 was eventually lost whilst flying with reserve-manned VFP-206 in the USA on 18 August 1973, but BuNo 145645 survived to be retired by VFP-63 to Davis-Monthan on 12 May 1982

**8**

Lt Cdr Schulze (kneeling with mascot) poses with the officers of his det (VFP-63 Det B) aboard *Hancock* in 1967. Standing, from left to right, are Ens John J Czekanski (PIO), Lt Bill D Stiehman (CVW-5 flight surgeon), Lt(jg) E H Haffey (senior PIO), Lt Ron F Ball, Lt Colin M Clark and Lt(jg) L E Johnson

**9**

This view of the VPAF airfield at Kep in 1967 shows revetments housing a few aircraft. The photo was probably taken by an F-4 crewman with a hand-held camera because RF-8s seldom went as far north as Kep, near the border with China

**10**

A railroad and highway bridge in Haiphong receives attention from CVW-15 strikes in 1967. While these strikes could have helped bring the Communists to the peace talks much sooner, the incomprehensible bombing halt instituted on 1 November 1968 by US President Johnson undid everything the intense bombing campaign had accomplished, and kept the war going for at least another four years

**11**

An RF-8G from *Coral Sea* took this BDA (Battle Damage Assessment) shot after CVW-15 strikes near Haiphong. BDA was the RF-8's 'bread and butter', and because of the predictability of its role after the strike, the photo-Crusader could usually expect a hot reception from gun and SAM batteries

**12**

NL 710 (BuNo 144618) hurtles down the track of the waist catapult during a launch from the *Coral Sea* in 1967. A Vietnam survivor, this aircraft has been a resident of Davis-Monthan AFB's AMARC facility since its retirement from VFP-63 on 15 April 1982

**13**

RF-8G BuNo 145627 of VFP-63's 'Home Guard' flies over the Sierra Nevada Mountains, this aircraft having also been a part of AMARC since 1 February 1982

**14**

RF-8G BuNo 146858 flies over the pine-covered Sierras in 1972 during a training mission. A veteran of numerous Vietnam cruises, this aircraft survived to be retired to Davis-Monthan by VFP-63 on 10 May 1982. Its time in the desert was ended on 5 February 1988, however, when it was acquired by the Marine Corps Air-Ground Museum at Quantico, in Virginia, who in turn loaned it MCAS El Toro, on the outskirts of Los Angeles. Today, it is one of a handful of ex-USMC jets proudly displayed near the main gate to the base, although with the imminent closure of this historic facility, its long-term future is presently in the balance

**15**

Shown during a pre-cruise training flight over the California Sierras, this immaculately marked RF-8G (BuNo 146892) is from the *Hancock* det. Note how its red bands and white stars on the wingtips and tail are echoed by the pilot's helmet decoration. In typical Crusader driver fashion, he has stashed his charts in between the forward windscreen and instrument panel. Since most *Hancock* RF-8 dets used a blue or black band throughout the 1960s, it could be assumed this photo shows the det colouring that showed up during the 1971 cruise. BuNo 146892 later became the second of eight VFP-63 photo-Crusaders lost in 1976-77, crashing on 15 July 1976

**16**

Flying over a picturesque setting in the California mountains, this RF-8G displays *Hancock* det colours on its tail and ventral strakes. The strakes, though large, handy areas, were not always used for such decorations. This jet was assigned to the unit's colourful commanding officer, Cdr J M Schulze, at the time, and it carries the '01' modex, prefixed by VFP-63's familiar number '9'. BuNo 146876 was the first photo-bird lost by VFP-63 during its infamous 'black' spell in 1976-77, the jet crashing on 1 June 1976

**17A**

Crusader shoulder patch, which was usually worn on a pilot's flight jacket, but also occasionally on flight suits, too

**17B**

The *Peanuts* beagle, *Snoopy*, was a popular mascot among the photo dets. Here, he rides a rather inaccurate caricature of a SAM

**17C**

Det Eleven served aboard USS *Intrepid* in 1967 and 1968. The Warner Brothers cartoon *Roadrunner* character was another oft-used symbol in squadron emblems

**17D**

*Oriskany*'s CVW-16 offered this rather nondescript patch. The distinctive flight deck of the 27C carrier is, however, noteworthy